OECD Development Co-operation Peer Reviews: Czech Republic 2016

This work is published under the responsibility of the Secretary-General of the OECD. The opinions expressed and arguments employed herein do not necessarily reflect the official views of OECD member countries.

This document and any map included herein are without prejudice to the status of or sovereignty over any territory, to the delimitation of international frontiers and boundaries and to the name of any territory, city or area.

Please cite this publication as:
OECD (2016), *OECD Development Co-operation Peer Reviews: Czech Republic 2016*, OECD Publishing, Paris.
http://dx.doi.org/10.1787/9789264264939-en

ISBN 978-92-64-26492-2 (print)
ISBN 978-92-64-26493-9 (PDF)

Series: OECD Development Co-operation Peer Reviews
ISSN 2309-7124 (print)
ISSN 2309-7132 (online)

The statistical data for Israel are supplied by and under the responsibility of the relevant Israeli authorities. The use of such data by the OECD is without prejudice to the status of the Golan Heights, East Jerusalem and Israeli settlements in the West Bank under the terms of international law.

Corrigenda to OECD publications may be found on line at: *www.oecd.org/about/publishing/corrigenda.htm*.

Conducting the peer review

The OECD Development Assistance Committee (DAC) conducts periodic reviews of the individual development co-operation efforts of DAC members. The policies and programmes of each member are critically examined approximately once every five years. Five members are examined annually. The OECD Development Co-operation Directorate provides analytical support, and develops and maintains, in close consultation with the Committee, the methodology and analytical framework – known as the Reference Guide – within which the peer reviews are undertaken.

The objectives of DAC peer reviews are to improve the quality and effectiveness of development co-operation policies and systems, and to promote good development partnerships for better impact on poverty reduction and sustainable development in developing countries. DAC peer reviews assess the performance of a given member, not just that of its development co-operation agency, and examine both policy and implementation. They take an integrated, system-wide perspective on the development co-operation and humanitarian assistance activities of the member under review.

The peer review is prepared by a team, consisting of representatives of the Secretariat working with officials from two DAC members who are designated as "examiners". The country under review provides a memorandum setting out the main developments in its policies and programmes. Then the Secretariat and the examiners visit the capital to interview officials, parliamentarians, as well as civil society and non-governmental organisations representatives of the donor country to obtain a first-hand insight into current issues surrounding the development co-operation efforts of the member concerned. Field visits assess how members are implementing the major DAC policies, principles and concerns, and review operations in recipient countries, particularly with regard to poverty reduction, sustainability, gender equality and other aspects of participatory development, and local aid co-ordination. During the field visit, the team meets with representatives of the partner country's administration, parliamentarians, civil society and other development partners.

The Secretariat then prepares a draft report on the member's development co-operation which is the basis for the DAC review meeting at the OECD. At this meeting senior officials from the member under review respond to questions formulated by the Committee in association with the examiners.

This review contains the main findings and recommendations of the Development Assistance Committee and the report of the Secretariat. It was prepared with examiners from the Netherlands and Switzerland for the peer review of the Czech Republic on 14 September 2016.

Table of contents

Tables

Figures

Boxes

Abbreviations and acronyms

CERF	Central Emergency Response Fund
COHAFA	Council Working Party on Humanitarian Aid and Food Aid
CPA	Country programmable aid
CRS	Creditor Reporting System
CzDA	Czech Development Agency
DAC	Development Assistance Committee
EC	European Commission
EU	European Union
FoRS	Czech Forum for Development Co-operation
GDP	Gross domestic product
GHD	Good Humanitarian Donorship
GNI	Gross national income
ICRC	International Committee of the Red Cross
LDCs	Least developed countries
MFA	Ministry of Foreign Affairs
MoFED	Ministry of Finance and Economic Development
MoI	Ministry of Interior
MoU	Memoranda of understanding
NGO	Non-governmental organisation
OCHA	United Nations Office for the Coordination of Humanitarian Affairs
ODA	Official development assistance
OECD	Organization for Economic Co-operation and Development
PCD	Policy coherence for development
PRT	Provincial Reconstruction Team
SDGs	Sustainable Development Goals
SNNPR	Southern Nations, Nationalities, and Peoples' Region
UN	United Nations
UNDP	United Nations Development Programme
UN-Habitat	United Nations Human Settlements Programme
UNHCR	United Nations High Commissioner for Refugees

Signs used:

CZK	Czech crowns
EUR	Euro
USD	United States dollars
( )	Secretariat estimate in whole or part
-	(Nil)
0.0	Negligible
..	Not available
...	Not available separately, but included in total
n.a.	Not applicable
p	Provisional

Slight discrepancies in totals are due to rounding.

Annual average exchange rate: 1 USD = CZK

2010	2011	2012	2013	2014	2015
19.0795	17.6722	19.5383	19.5585	20.7578	24.5926

The Czech Republic's aid at a glance

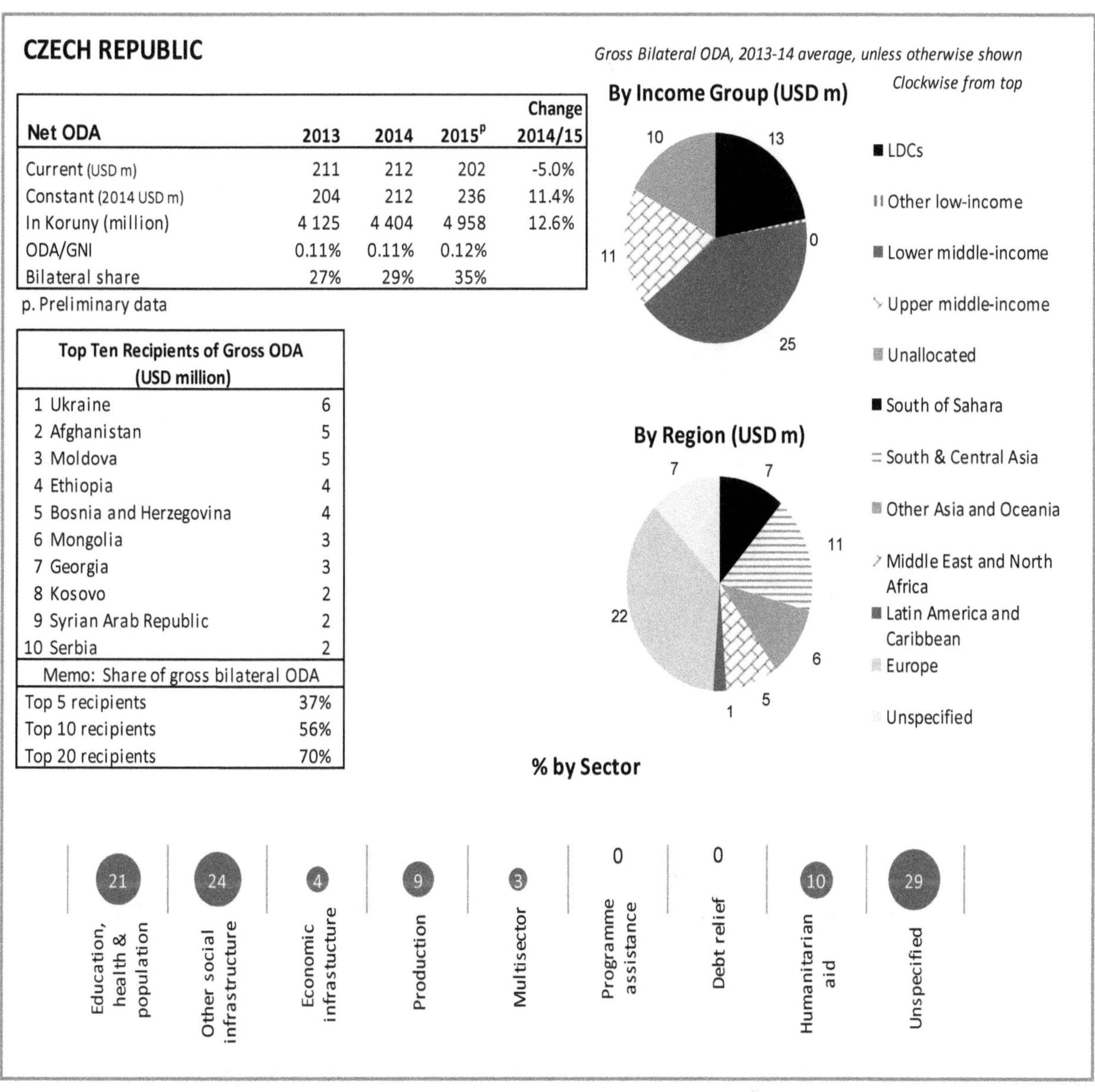

CZECH REPUBLIC

Net ODA	2013	2014	2015p	Change 2014/15
Current (USD m)	211	212	202	-5.0%
Constant (2014 USD m)	204	212	236	11.4%
In Koruny (million)	4 125	4 404	4 958	12.6%
ODA/GNI	0.11%	0.11%	0.12%	
Bilateral share	27%	29%	35%	

p. Preliminary data

Top Ten Recipients of Gross ODA (USD million)	
1 Ukraine	6
2 Afghanistan	5
3 Moldova	5
4 Ethiopia	4
5 Bosnia and Herzegovina	4
6 Mongolia	3
7 Georgia	3
8 Kosovo	2
9 Syrian Arab Republic	2
10 Serbia	2
Memo: Share of gross bilateral ODA	
Top 5 recipients	37%
Top 10 recipients	56%
Top 20 recipients	70%

Source: OECD-DAC; www.oecd.org/dac/stats

Context of the peer review of the Czech Republic

The Czech Republic has a population of about 10.5 million and its gross domestic product (GDP) per capita was USD 32 675 in 2015 (OECD, 2016a). Its current government was formed at the beginning of 2014. It is made up of a three-party coalition led by the Czech Social Democratic Party and including the Christian and Democratic Union, known as the Czechoslovak People's Party, and ANO – a new political movement.

The OECD's 2016 Economic Survey of the Czech Republic noted that economic growth picked up strongly in 2015, with GDP growing by 4.3% (compared to 1.9% in 2014). This was driven by strengthening private consumption, as well as a boost from EU-financed public investment. In 2016 economic growth is projected to slow down at 2.4% due to falling public investment, reflecting lower disbursement of EU structural funds. The Czech unemployment rate has decreased steadily since 2013 and is now below the OECD estimate of full employment – at 6% at the end of 2015. It is projected to decrease further in 2016 and 2017 (OECD, 2016b).

How's Life in the Czech Republic shows that the Czech Republic has one of the highest level of educational attainment in the OECD. It has one of the lowest average household disposable incomes per capita in the OECD and low average earnings. However, in terms of job security, Czech employees are less likely to lose their jobs than the average OECD employee (OECD, 2015).

A key challenge for the Czech economy will be to reduce the high energy and carbon intensity of its growth by shifting away from coal and improving energy efficiency. While subsidies and grants for investment in renewable energy and improving energy efficiency have been expanded, the effective tax rate on CO_2 emissions remains low in comparison to other OECD countries.

The Czech Republic's foreign policy, like in other EU member states, has been focusing, among other issues, on the ongoing refugee and migration crisis in Europe. The Czech Republic participates in the EU voluntary quota scheme and has agreed to resettle 942 refugees in 2016 and 1 749 in 2017. It continues to liaise closely with Visegrad and Western Balkan countries on migration. Economic diplomacy has also become a bigger priority in foreign policy. These two aspects of foreign policy also influence Czech development co-operation policy.

The 2010-2017 Development Cooperation Strategy of the Czech Republic has helped to take forward a new era of Czech development co-operation, which included joining the Development Assistance Committee (DAC) in 2013. This is the first development co-operation peer review of the Czech Republic. There are therefore no recommendations from previous DAC peer reviews against which to assess Czech progress. However, the peer review holds the Czech Republic accountable for the commitments it has made domestically and internationally. Being a first peer review, a strong emphasis is placed on learning and on setting a baseline for Czech development co-operation in the future.

Sources:

OECD (2016a), Gross domestic product (GDP) (indicator), DOI: http://dx.doi.org/10.1787/dc2f7aec-en, accessed 10 May 2016.

OECD, (2016b), OECD Economic Surveys: Czech Republic 2016, OECD Publishing, Paris, DOI: http://dx.doi.org/10.1787/eco_surveys-cze-2016-en.

OECD (2015), "How's life in the Czech Republic?", October 2015, www.oecd.org/czech/Better%20Life%20Initiative%20country%20note%20Czech%20Republic.pdf.

The DAC's main findings and recommendations

1 Towards a comprehensive Czech development effort

Indicator: The member has a broad, strategic approach to development and financing for development beyond aid. This is reflected in overall policies, co-ordination within its government system and operations

Main findings

The Czech Republic achieved a significant milestone as a provider of development assistance when it joined the Development Assistance Committee (DAC) in 2013. Since then it has continued to strengthen its support for development and global public policy processes for "peace, people, prosperity and planet". This strong commitment to development is enabled by broad political and public support.

As a DAC member, the Czech Republic has pledged to fulfil the committee's obligations and to meet international development commitments and standards. This first DAC Peer Review of the Czech Republic establishes a baseline and direction of travel for its development co-operation over the medium term. This review also illustrates the impressive progress that the Czech Republic has made to strengthen its strategic framework, institutional system and structures for quality development co-operation.

The Czech Republic participates actively and strategically in the global system for sustainable development. It brings credible lessons and experience to international forums which stem from its own transition experience and its growing development co-operation expertise. The issues for which it advocates – human rights, gender equality and good governance – are in line with its foreign policy and track record, which are founded on a strong conviction that these are essential for functioning democracies.

It was in this spirit that the Czech Republic consistently raised the flag for Sustainable Development Goal (SDG) 16 to promote just, peaceful and inclusive societies during the Agenda 2030 negotiations and joined the "HeForShe" campaign when it celebrated 70 years of UN membership in 2015. Through its active support for the European Union's Neighbourhood Policy and integration process, it is helping other countries who are now transitioning to democracy and market economies.

Integrating Agenda 2030 into national policy is driven from the highest political level, by the Government Council for Sustainable Development chaired by the Prime Minister. This should give the future Framework for Sustainable Development the required weight across government.

Agenda 2030 - and national efforts to implement it - is a major opportunity for the Czech Republic to reposition its commitment to policy coherence for development in domestic policy discussions and as an integral part of delivering the SDGs.

The Council for Development Cooperation, chaired by the Deputy Minister for Development Cooperation, has the potential to play a more active role in raising awareness across government of how the Czech Republic's policies could be more development-friendly. However, at present this council does not have a clear mandate for pursuing policy coherence for development.

Multi-stakeholder analyses of cases of (in)coherent policies could help to enhance understanding of how the Czech Republic can deliver on its commitment to policy coherence for development. For example, Czech civil society, including its universities and think tanks, is a key asset for the Czech Republic. It could draw further on the capacity and expertise within civil society and other organisations, such as the OECD, to step up analysis and monitoring of the coherence of Czech policies with development.

The Czech Republic is developing instruments to use official development assistance (ODA) to encourage other types of investment in development. For example, technical assistance on public finance management and the Aid for Trade programme help partner countries or territories improve budgetary processes and trade performance. However, a challenge for the government is to help Czech businesses understand the potential of investing in sustainable development and how they can become partners for development rather than aid contractors. The Czech Business Platform for Development Cooperation would be a useful forum for defining a private sector strategy.

Recommendation

1.1 The Czech Republic's national strategic framework for Agenda 2030, its target setting and annual monitoring should address the global dimensions of the SDGs.

1.2 To help it deliver policies that are coherent with the aspirations of developing countries, the Czech Republic should draw more on its national expertise for policy analysis and to increase awareness of the impact of Czech policies on developing countries.

1.3 The Czech Republic should define a private sector partnership strategy that helps Czech businesses understand the potential of investing in sustainable development as partners rather than as aid contractors.

2 The Czech Republic's vision and policies for development co-operation

Indicator: Clear political directives, policies and strategies shape the member's development co-operation and are in line with international commitments and guidance

Main findings

The Czech Republic has a clear, broadly owned policy vision and strategy for development co-operation, which is considered an integral part of its foreign policy. According to the 2010 Act on Development Cooperation and Humanitarian Aid, Czech development co-operation should "contribute to eradicating poverty in the context of sustainable development, [and contribute] to economic and social development, environmental protection, and promoting democracy, human rights and good governance in developing countries".

The Czech Republic has a strong comparative advantage, particularly in its co-operation with partner countries in the Western Balkans and Eastern Europe: it draws on the experience and knowledge gained from transitioning to democracy and a market economy. This was apparent in the field perspective from Moldova.

The Czech Republic has a solid vision and growing practical experience that can be used to strengthen its development co-operation under the next medium-term strategy – to be finalised in 2017. It also has strengths and opportunities that it can draw on as it develops the new strategy. It can, for example:

- leverage further the current political commitment to Agenda 2030 to position development co-operation policy firmly in the domestic debate on the sustainable development goals and within foreign policy.
- capitalise on its evolving comparative advantage in sharing its transition experience by identifying more explicitly how to transfer knowledge, often tacit, and make clearer the links between this comparative advantage and the poverty reduction objectives of the development act.
- develop a niche approach to maximise its value-added in least developed partner countries or territories where Czech aid makes up a relatively small share of total aid and public finance for development.
- gain more policy influence in multilateral settings, including the EU, by leveraging its financial contributions and expertise to advance priority themes globally and locally (e.g. governance and institution building). Its leadership could be strengthened by being more focused and strategic about what it can achieve through its multilateral contributions to achieve the SDGs.

One of the main strategic challenges that the Czech Republic needs to manage carefully is priority setting. Given the limited size of its aid budget, there are too many geographic and thematic priorities in the current strategy. At the same time, there are growing demands on the Czech Republic to use its ODA to respond to new foreign policy and political imperatives, such as instability in the region (e.g. Ukraine) and the ongoing refugee crisis. Czech ODA is also fragmented within its partner countries or territories: relatively small budgets are spread across several sectors and stand-alone projects. Impact and sustainability could be increased by focusing on those themes where it can add value, maximising synergies among activities and working in a more programmatic way. The government's plans for the next strategy – to focus bilateral ODA on only six countries, and on themes where it can add value – are a move in the right direction.

The overall strategic framework could be better supported by guidance in specific areas. While there is evidence that Czech aid targets vulnerability and inequalities in Moldova and Ethiopia, there is no specific guidance for focusing on poverty reduction. It is hard to say how systematically it focuses on the neediest. Clearer guidelines and political leadership could also help mainstream cross-cutting priorities into programmes and policy dialogue.

Recommendations

2.1 The Czech Republic should integrate development co-operation into its national plan for delivering on Agenda 2030, and into the domestic debate and institutional set-up on sustainable development.

2.2 To continue to increase the quality and impact of its aid, the Czech Republic should focus on fewer partner countries or territories and themes, deliver on its comparative advantage and maximise synergies for greater impact.

2.3 The Ministry of Foreign Affairs (MFA) should provide clear objectives and policy guidance for delivering on strategic priorities such as poverty reduction, social and economic transition and cross-cutting issues.

3 Allocating the Czech Republic's official development assistance

Indicator: The member's international and national commitments drive aid volume and allocations

Main findings

In 2015 the Czech Republic's net ODA was USD 236 million (in constant 2014 prices) – an increase of 11.4% in real terms compared to 2014 (USD 212 million). Its ratio of ODA to gross national income also rose: to 0.12% from 0.11% in 2014. Czech ODA levels still have some distance to go to reach the target of providing 0.33% of national income as ODA by 2030 (to which the Czech Republic re-committed in the 2015 Addis Ababa Action Agenda). However, there are positive political signals and a conducive macro-economic context for achieving intended increases to reach a target of 0.17% ODA/GNI by 2020. These trends should enable the Czech Republic to deliver a more ambitious plan for reaching the 0.33% target.

The 2014 and 2015 aid increases reverse a declining trend in bilateral aid which decreased by USD 49 million between 2008 and 2013 and reflect plans to scale up bilateral aid. Given the relatively small size of bilateral aid (USD 71 million, 2015 preliminary), the Czech Republic has decided to use the budget increases up to 2020 to scale-up the bilateral portfolio. The Czech Government has endorsed an annual increase of CZK 100 million (approximately USD 4 million) for bilateral development assistance and humanitarian aid in 2017-2019.

In 2015 multilateral aid accounted for 65% (preliminary data) of total Czech ODA and is mostly assessed contributions to the European Union (82% of multilateral contributions in 2015). The Czech Republic targets its limited earmarked contributions strategically such as through trust funds that align with its priorities.

Since joining the DAC, the Czech Republic has also made significant progress in reporting its ODA flows according to DAC rules. More comprehensive, detailed and timely statistical reporting has increased the transparency of its aid. By sharing its forward-spending plans on ODA, it has increased predictability for its partners. This is good practice.

The Czech Republic uses its annual development co-operation plan to ensure that aid is allocated according to its strategic priorities. According to this plan and DAC data, Czech bilateral aid allocations reflect its geographical and sectoral priorities: in 2013-2014, 8 of its 11 priority countries or territories were among its top 10 aid recipients. The sectoral focus was on education, and governance and civil society (although the latter declined to 13% of bilateral aid in 2013-2014 from 28% in 2008-12), water supply and sanitation and agriculture (both receiving 8%). Humanitarian aid accounted for 10% of bilateral aid in 2013-14. While aid to in-donor refugee costs fell slightly in 2013-2014, its overall share of bilateral ODA increased from 14% in 2008-12 to 18% in 2013-2014 due to the fall in bilateral aid.

The Czech Republic prioritises efficiency, impact and sustainability when allocating aid. However, it needs to allocate aid to fewer priorities overall and to have more focused programmes in partner countries or territories. For example, with 46 activities in Moldova in 2014 and a total budget of USD 5 million, most disbursements were less than USD 100 000. Partners in Ethiopia and Moldova flagged the need for it to increase scale to raise impact. The Czech Development Agency (CzDA) implemented 123 projects with a total budget of USD 17.6 million in 2014.

If, as planned in the next medium-term strategy, the bilateral aid budget increases, the number of priority countries or territories declines to six and the Czech Republic focuses on no more than three sectors in priority countries or territories, it will be in a position to increase the budget envelope for its priority countries or territories and consequently engage in longer-term and more concerted programmes. Integrating the technical assistance provided by a range of Czech ministries into a more programmatic approach can also reinforce synergies among projects and help increase the impact and visibility of the country or territory's comparative advantage.

Recommendations

3.1 Building on the momentum created by the recent increase in ODA towards 0.17% ODA/GNI by 2020, the Czech Republic should have a more ambitious plan and time-line for reaching the target of 0.33% ODA/GNI.

3.2 The Czech Republic should use its increase in bilateral aid to achieve a critical mass, broader scale and impact in partner countries or territories, including by taking a more programmatic approach.

4 Managing the Czech Republic's development co-operation

Indicator: The member's approach to how it organises and manages its development co-operation is fit for purpose

Main findings

Since joining the DAC in 2013 the Czech Republic has continued to strengthen its institutional system and structures to deliver quality development co-operation. The Supreme Audit Office confirmed in its audit that the system is managed well, is functional and efficient.

The Czech Republic has built up several assets which are conducive to ensuring its development co-operation is organised and managed for delivering quality aid. These include the MFA's solid political and strategic leadership; the inter-ministerial Council for Development Cooperation, which helps build ownership of the programme; and the Czech Development Agency.

The Ministry of Foreign Affairs' position as institutional leader of Czech development co-operation has been consolidated by creating one main budget line which it administers. The MFA is well-placed to steer aid planning and programming within the overall medium-term strategy and annual spending plans.

The Czech Development Agency (CzDA) is recognised as a capable implementing body with solid procedures and good project management. The project cycle manual, for example, is a useful and adaptable tool for a systematic and transparent approach. The Agency has the capacity to absorb a larger aid budget.

The CzDA plans to decentralise staff to the field, starting with Ethiopia in 2016. With a stronger field presence, it will be better placed to respond to partner country or territory needs and to harmonise with other providers. It may also free up time for the embassy's development diplomats to participate more actively in policy dialogue, in line with the embassy's mandate. To implement these objectives effectively, the MFA will need to ensure a clear division of labour between embassy and agency staff in partner countries or territories, provide strategic direction and guidance, and give appropriate decentralised decision-making and financial authority.

As the Czech system continues to develop and consolidate, it needs to identify and adapt the rules and procedures which restrict the Agency's and other implementing bodies' flexibility to choose the most appropriate instrument to deliver the programme and engage in partnerships. For example, the requirement to deliver grants through entities registered in the Czech Republic, such as NGOs and businesses, limits the scope of the activities that the Czech Republic can support.

Human resource capacity gaps are a key vulnerability in the Czech system. At present, human resources at the Department for Development Cooperation and Humanitarian Aid are stretched, with individual staff managing several large policy, programming and technical (e.g. evaluation and statistics) portfolios at once. This is hindering the department's ability to advance strategic priorities related to Agenda 2030, to elevate development co-operation as a key pillar of foreign policy, to facilitate more strategic whole-of-government approaches in partner countries or territories, and to deliver policy guidance to the Development Agency.

While staffing levels and capacity have increased in the Agency, it still lacks sufficient capacity in precise areas (e.g. procurement, risk management, cross-cutting issues) and it needs to ensure that capacity in headquarters is not undermined by sending staff to partner countries or territories.

Line ministries also face a capacity challenge in managing and responding to increased demands from developing countries (and international organisations) for transition-related technical assistance. The Czech Development Agency is starting to play a facilitating role, which could be developed further provided the Czech Republic has a clear strategy for how it will capitalise on this type of technical assistance.

Finally, there is also scope for the MFA to integrate the specific staffing needs of the development co-operation programme into its human resource management – notably when rotating staff and through more tailor-made training.

Recommendations

4.1 The Czech Republic should identify ways to have appropriate human resource capacity in the right place across the development co-operation system and to ensure staff have the skills and expertise needed to deliver the programme efficiently and effectively.

4.2 Decentralisation to the field should be backed by appropriate authority for embassy and agency staff, as well as clear roles and responsibilities.

5 The Czech Republic's development co-operation delivery and partnerships

Indicator: The member's approach to how it delivers its programme leads to quality assistance in partner countries or territories, maximizing the impact of its support, as defined in Busan

Main findings

The Czech Republic is committed to the principles of effective development co-operation agreed in the Busan Partnership. For example, its multi-year indicative budgets give predictability to partners and it identifies and aligns to partner country or territory needs through active dialogue as found in Moldova.

The Ministry of Foreign Affairs and the Czech Development Agency have gained experience and lessons from ongoing country programmes, notably on setting fewer and clearer priorities. These will inform the next round of programmes. The Agency continues to refine project procedures through experience and feedback from NGOs and embassy staff. According to the Supreme Audit Office's audit, project design is becoming better focused on sustainable impact.

The same audit also found that formal bilateral agreements with partner countries or territories would strengthen Czech co-operation and mutual accountability. Current memoranda of understanding with partner governments do not have legal status, which can limit ownership.

Given its limited resources and capacity in the field, the Czech Republic is pragmatic in how it partners with other donors: it focuses on division of labour, EU joint programming and, when it can, leading sector work. For example, in Moldova, it leads the joint analysis of the social sectors. The planned decentralisation of CzDA staff is an opportunity to deepen partnerships and the visibility of Czech aid through more harmonised arrangements. It could also gain from the knowledge and experience that is often shared between providers through co-ordination and dialogue.

Czech NGOs are an asset and major partner for delivering ODA. They also play an important watchdog role, challenging the government to deliver on its aid targets and commitments. Several Czech NGOs and their local partners have built up a good track record and capacity. However, the Agency still allocates grants to NGOs through calls for project proposals rather than through strategic partnerships. There is scope to develop a strategic framework for partnering with civil society and to use more effective funding mechanisms for Czech and non-Czech organisations, in line with Busan indicator two.

The Agency's medium-term vision states that the Czech Republic needs to re-think its aid modalities to maximise its impact in partner countries or territories. The current project approach reduces flexibility and carries high administrative costs. For example, although it is increasingly supporting multi-year rather than annual projects, the Agency has to prepare a new contract for each year of the project and financial rules require detailed reporting and proof of expenditure for all projects and tenders, no matter the size.

A more thorough approach to assessing and managing the risks and opportunities in achieving development results could reinforce the evidence-base for programme design and for choosing the most appropriate aid modalities. Since the Czech Republic delivers aid in fragile states, there is also scope for more systematic and joint analysis with partners of the drivers of fragility, including climate change, to inform policy dialogue and programmes.

Legally, ODA must be channelled to partner countries or territories through entities registered in the Czech Republic. As a result, only 32.4% of Czech aid was untied in 2014. While the MFA and the Agency are identifying changes required to untie aid further, they also need to convince the government and key stakeholders that untying aid increases value for money and local ownership. According to OECD research, tied aid "can increase the costs of a development project by as much as 15 to 30 per cent."

The rules for channelling aid through Czech entities make it difficult for the Agency to use partner systems. However, it could do more to use and strengthen country systems by, for example, ensuring aid is on budget even if it cannot use country financial systems for disbursement. It could also become a niche provider within programme-based approaches and integrate projects and technical assistance into the programmes.

Recommendations

5.1 The Czech Republic should have a vision and policy for strategic partnerships with civil society for development co-operation and develop an appropriate mix of funding mechanisms.

5.2 The Czech Republic should update its rules and procedures so that it can untie aid, use partner systems, and contribute to harmonised funding arrangements in line with Busan commitments.

6 Results management and accountability of Czech development co-operation

Indicator: The member plans and manages for results, learning, transparency and accountability

Main findings

Managing for development results is a growing priority for the Czech Republic. Over the past few years it has focused on having a robust and results-oriented approach to project management. There is a positive culture of learning: reviews, monitoring and evaluations are used to improve the quality and management of development interventions.

These are good foundations on which to build a more comprehensive results-based management system that links results from projects and programmes to strategic objectives. This should ensure that it is getting the most out of its investments. By improving the quality of programmes and by learning from results information, the Czech Republic will also be better placed to communicate its impacts, such as on achieving the SDGs, to parliament and the public.

The Czech Development Agency and the Ministry of Foreign Affairs recognise that managing for development results is still a work in progress. Experience from other DAC members shows that institutionalising a results culture requires leadership from the top to build a common vision. It also requires information on results for decision making and accountability – to taxpayers and beneficiaries. This demands technical capacity for results planning, measuring and monitoring. In rising to this challenge, the Czech Republic could learn from and share experience through the DAC Results Community.

Plans and investments at the MFA and the Agency for developing more strategic and targeted communication about development co-operation respond to the need for a better-informed public. The Czech Republic also invests in global education through a collaborative strategy implemented by the MFA; the Ministry of Education, Youth and Sports; the Agency and Czech NGOs.

By institutionalising evaluation throughout the system, the MFA plans to use it to improve the quality and management of development interventions. It has a dedicated Evaluation Unit, a specific budget and an annual evaluation plan which is discussed by the Evaluation Working Group of the Council for Development Cooperation. It is then approved by the Council and published on the MFA's website.

The MFA has taken a number of steps to maintain the credibility of its evaluation function in a resource-constrained environment. It commissions independent evaluators, benefits from the evaluation oversight role played by the Council for Development Cooperation, and has a reference group of experts for each evaluation. However, the independence of the evaluation function from policy and programming could be reinforced within the MFA. There is a risk, under the current reporting line, of a conflict of interest between policy, programming and evaluation.

The purpose, procedures, role and responsibilities for evaluation are outlined in the project cycle methodology, but this tends to narrow the evaluation function to programming and projects. Having an overall evaluation policy could help to set out the institutional arrangements needed to ensure independence and clarify the overall strategic purpose and role of evaluation in Czech development co-operation. Finally, with just one staff member working on evaluation (as well as other duties), the MFA can only manage three to six evaluations a year. Capacity is therefore limited for strengthening the role of evaluation across the system – whether as a tool for evidence-based decision making, to test strategies and innovation, or build a learning culture.

The Czech Republic has improved the transparency of its aid through statistical reporting and by publishing a broad range of information on its website. It can continue to make progress by publishing information according to the Busan Common Standard, but needs first to fix technical problems with its data management system.

Recommendations

6.1 The Czech Republic should develop a more comprehensive approach to managing for results at the strategic, programme and project levels aligning with the SDGs and partner country or territory results frameworks.

6.2 The Czech Republic should ensure it has adequate capacity for managing evaluations, guarantee their independence, and use them for evidence-based decisions and accountability.

7 The Czech Republic's humanitarian assistance

Indicator: The member contributes to minimising impact of shocks and crises; and saves lives, alleviates suffering and maintains human dignity in crisis and disaster settings

Main findings

Since 2010, the Czech Republic has made good progress implementing its humanitarian policy framework. Its humanitarian strategy is driven by international humanitarian laws, the Good Humanitarian Donorship principles and the EU consensus on humanitarian aid.

The 2010-2017 Development Cooperation Strategy provides a broad framework for Czech involvement in humanitarian assistance, referring to disaster risk reduction, the links between relief and development and climate change adaptation. The strategy also defines humanitarian aid as the first step after a crisis. However, the Czech Republic's practical experience with protracted crises in Ukraine and the Middle East shows that in some contexts humanitarian and development assistance need to be provided simultaneously. Based on this experience, the Czech Republic could usefully reinforce its holistic approach in the new development co-operation framework.

The Czech Republic has endorsed the Grand Bargain – a key outcome of the 2016 World Humanitarian Summit. The provisions of the Grand Bargain should inform the Czech Republic's upcoming humanitarian strategy.

The Czech Republic's humanitarian budget has been stable since 2010 at about CZK 73 million (USD 3 million) a year. Since 2014, the humanitarian budget received additional allocations to respond to specific crises such as Ukraine and the Ebola outbreak. In 2015, these allocations increased the initial budget by 23%.

The Czech Republic has ambitious objectives for humanitarian assistance but a limited budget. This creates a risk of spreading funding too thinly across several crises. The MFA selects its humanitarian partners and the programmes to fund strategically, with a focus on the underfunded humanitarian work of multilateral organisations. This niche approach is relevant and could be strengthened, allowing the Czech Republic to maximise its limited humanitarian resources while keeping control over programme design. By further developing the comparative advantage of its humanitarian funding in response to humanitarian crises, the Czech Republic could increase focus and strengthen links with other donors, in the spirit of the Grand Bargain.

Projects by NGOs registered in the Czech Republic are selected for funding through an annual call for proposals. While the government's financial contribution is small, NGO partners value the legitimacy they get from its support, which can open doors to other funding, such as from the EU. Reporting requirements on implementing partners are not burdensome.

However, humanitarian funding allocated to priority countries or territories is fragmented; this puts a substantial administrative burden on the individual staff member managing this portfolio at the MFA. Financial rules that dictate a quarterly disbursement of the budget also make financial planning difficult for the Czech Republic's partners.

The Czech Republic uses the EU early warning mechanism and works closely with its representatives in Rome, Geneva, Brussels and New York to ensure early updates on crisis evolution. This allows for a rapid and co-ordinated response, especially to natural disasters, as witnessed during the 2014 Balkans floods and the 2015 Nepal earthquake. It co-ordinates with other donors as part of the Council working party on Humanitarian Aid and Food Aid.

New crisis patterns blur the clear distinction between humanitarian action, development, security and migration management. This brings some challenges for which the Czech Republic must be prepared. The MFA and the Ministry of Interior have a solid co-ordination mechanism when responding to disasters. This co-operation could be extended to migration management to ensure that the Czech Republic's assistance remains bound to humanitarian principles.

Recommendations

7.1 The Czech Republic should focus on its comparative advantage in humanitarian assistance by further developing its niche approach; this would help maximise its effectiveness and influence while increasing its scope for co-operation with other donors.

7.2 The Czech Republic should focus its humanitarian funding on fewer crises and rationalise its funding calendar to better match its administrative capacity.

Secretariat's report

Chapter 1: Towards a comprehensive Czech development effort

Global development issues

The Czech Republic participates actively in international efforts to promote and implement development-relevant global public policies. It places a strong emphasis on human rights, good governance and gender equality. Another key priority of its foreign policy is to support the European Union's Neighbourhood Policy and integration process. The 2030 Agenda for Sustainable Development is being integrated into national policy through the work of the Government Council for Sustainable Development – i.e. at the highest political level. The Czech Republic should ensure that the national plan for the Sustainable Development Goals (SDGs) integrates international development, for example, by including indicators for policy coherence for sustainable development in the SDG monitoring framework.

The Czech Republic advocates globally for human rights, gender equality and good governance

Solving global issues requires that the role of official development assistance (ODA) be adapted and complemented by other substantial contributions, according to the Czech Republic (MFA, 2016). The Czech Republic contributes strategically, through channels other than ODA, to international efforts to implement development-relevant global public policies, including international security treaties. Within the European Union (EU), it provides political support to the integration process of southern European countries and to the EU Eastern Partnership policy.

The Czech Republic's foreign policy emphasises promoting human rights and democracy (MFA, 2015). During the inter-governmental negotiations for the 2030 Agenda for Sustainable Development, it advocated strongly for human rights and fundamental freedoms, gender equality and the empowerment of women and girls, good governance, respect of the rule of law, and effective and efficient institutions.[1] For example, it joined the 'HeForShe' campaign in June 2015 during the celebration of the 70th anniversary of the Czech Republic's membership of the UN. The Czech Republic is also an active player in the United Nations Human Rights Council.

The Czech Republic is actively engaged at the highest political level in promoting the 2030 Agenda for Sustainable Development (Box 1.1). In March 2016, it hosted the UN European Habitat Conference "Housing in Liveable Cities",[2] one of the first UN conferences focused on implementing the goals of the 2030 Agenda. The Czech Republic is currently updating its Strategic Sustainable Development Framework (GoCR, 2010), which will guide the implementation of the SDGs at the national level. It needs to ensure that this framework and the national action plan integrate the international dimension of sustainable development and recognise that the Czech Republic's domestic and international policies and efforts contribute to the SDGs nationally and globally.

Box 1.1 Active leadership in integrating the Sustainable Development Goals into national policy

The process for implementing the 2030 Agenda for Sustainable Development (UN, 2015) in the Czech Republic is led at the highest political level through the work of the Government Council for Sustainable Development which is chaired by the Prime Minister and supported by the Unit for Sustainable Development in the Office of the Government. This Council is co-ordinating efforts to integrate the Sustainable Development Goals (SDGs) into national policy. The Government Council for Sustainable Development is also playing a key role, acting as a suitable platform for discussions on inter-ministerial issues and cross-cutting agendas.

The Czech Republic is conducting a screening exercise to select a limited number of priority targets to be tracked at national level. It is updating and redefining the Czech Strategic Framework for Sustainable Development, which will be re-named "Czech Republic 2030". The government's objective is to achieve a sustainable quality of life for all. The framework will be submitted to the government at the end of 2016 and the Czech Republic plans to establish a two-year reporting mechanism on the state of sustainability in the country. The main challenge highlighted by the Czech Republic is the need for better guidance from international organisations, like the OECD, on how to analyse and link policy coherence for sustainable development and policy coherence for development. Other challenges are collecting disaggregated data and developing good indicators to monitor and measure progress.[3]

Source: Interviews conducted during the DAC Peer Review mission in Prague; the Czech Republic's intervention at the *OECD 2016 Global Forum on Development* (www.oecd.org/site/oecdgfd/); UN (2015), "Transforming our World: the 2030 Agenda for Sustainable Development", United Nations Resolution A/RES/70/1, 25 September 2015, https://sustainabledevelopment.un.org/post2015/transformingourworld/publication.

Policy coherence for development

Indicator: Domestic policies support or do not harm developing countries

The Czech Republic has committed to work on policy coherence for development (PCD) in its development co-operation strategy and has established mechanisms for inter-ministerial co-ordination. However, this commitment has not yet translated into concrete goals or practical steps. The Council for Development Cooperation does not have a mandate to discuss non-development policies and awareness of PCD is low across the administration. Efforts to integrate the 2030 Agenda into national policy present an opportunity to position policy coherence in a new way in domestic policy discussions and the institutional set-up; to identify, analyse, monitor and report cases of trade-offs between Czech policies and their impact on developing countries; and to establish a plan for addressing these issues. The expertise of domestic research institutes and non-governmental organisations is an important resource on which to draw.

Commitment to policy coherence for development now needs practical action

The Development Cooperation Strategy 2010-2017 (MFA, 2010) commits the Czech Republic to policy coherence for development (PCD), which is considered an important precondition for meeting development goals. The strategy states that "in accordance with the principles of the EU, UN and OECD, the Czech Republic will place emphasis (at both national and EU level) on Policy Coherence for Development" and will "ensure that the external impacts of departmental policies do not undermine the aims and objectives of development policy (especially in trade, agriculture, migration, environment and security)" (MFA, 2010).

Like many Development Assistance Committee (DAC) members, the Czech Republic can do more to improve the development-friendliness of its domestic and international policies. For example, the 2015 Commitment to Development Index[4] ranks the Czech Republic 18th out of 27 DAC countries, which is an improvement from its 22nd place in 2014.[5] However, with the exception of some analytical work on food security, it has not yet translated its commitment to policy coherence for development into a plan for action. The Czech Republic could, for example, identify whether its policies or policy positions in areas mentioned in the strategy (ibid) are development-friendly and agree on priority actions to take where it can make a difference, especially at the EU level, given the EU's competencies.

There is low awareness and understanding of policy coherence for development and the institutional mandate for delivering on the commitment is vague

The Czech Republic has several institutional mechanisms for co-ordinating cross-government policy positions.[6] When it comes to ensuring that domestic policies support, or at least do not have a negative impact on developing countries, the Council for Development Cooperation is "responsible for mutual coherence between the objectives and priorities of development co-operation and other government policy instruments that have or could have a direct or indirect impact on developing countries" (Council of Development Cooperation, 2008). As the government's focal point for policy coherence for development, the primary task of the Department of Development Cooperation and Humanitarian Assistance in the Ministry of Foreign Affairs (MFA) is to initiate and co-ordinate inter-ministerial dialogue within the Council and to facilitate civil society engagement in formulating and implementing strategies.

However, while the Council is responsible for promoting development-friendly policies, in practice it cannot fulfil this role: the Council is only mandated to discuss development co-operation policies. As a result, it focuses more on coherence within the development co-operation policy than on policy coherence for development.

There is also low awareness and understanding of policy coherence for development across the administration. The Council for Development Cooperation is striving to raise inter-ministerial and parliamentary awareness, but this is a challenge.[7] Awareness-raising activities include disseminating papers that address policy coherence for development and collaborating with Czech think-tanks, such as Glopolis, which have published numerous studies and reports on PCD and organised public debates.

The Czech Republic could step up efforts to deliver on its commitment to policy coherence for development. Agenda 2030 provides a good platform and opportunity to make progress given that it is driven by the Office of the Government. The Czech Republic could, for example, position PCD as an integral part of the forthcoming national SDG Action Plan (Box 1.1). It will also need a strategic plan with clear priorities and should give a strong mandate to a relevant institution that is capable of identifying potential for greater coherence, arbitrating when incoherence arises and monitoring and reporting on progress. Strong political leadership will also be essential for success.

Monitoring of the impact of Czech policies in developing countries is limited

At present, the Czech Republic does not conduct systematic analysis of the potential trade-offs between its national policies and development. According to its response to the questionnaire for the EU-Policy Coherence for Development Report 2015, development objectives are not taken into account by the government in assessing the impact of non-development policies, and there are no mechanisms or indicators to measure and evaluate the impact of national policies on developing countries or to evaluate and report on whether the government has implemented its commitment to PCD (EC, 2015a).

The Czech Republic can draw on strong analytical capacity outside government to identify inconsistent policies

Thorough multi-stakeholder analysis of cases of incoherence can be instrumental in enhancing the level of understanding of PCD and the trade-offs necessary to make it happen. In the past, the Czech Republic chose food security as a pilot theme for PCD analysis. The Ministry of Foreign Affairs and the Ministry of Agriculture commissioned Glopolis to study this theme. The study suggested practical measures for the government to implement in the area of agricultural trade and climate change to enhance the development-friendliness of its policies but there has been no formal follow-up by the government (Glopolis, 2012).

The Czech Republic can draw on the valuable expertise of its domestic research institutes by harnessing their analytical capacity to track the effect of various policies on development and to find practical examples of policies that are harmful for developing countries. Solid analysis linked with the advocacy power of Czech non-governmental organisations (NGOs), could be an important resource for increasing awareness and understanding within relevant ministries and Parliament of the impacts of national policies on developing countries. Raising awareness is fundamental to fostering political commitment to tackle incoherent policies.

Financing for development

Indicator: The member engages in development finance in addition to ODA

The Czech Republic recognises the role of ODA as a catalyst for mobilising other resources for sustainable development, including from the private sector. Further efforts are needed to identify how it can best support the development of the private sector in developing countries and how the Czech private sector can engage in development co-operation in line with development effectiveness principles. The creation of the Business Platform for Development is an opportunity to raise awareness of the development potential of private investment.

The Ministry of Foreign Affairs recognises the multiple roles of ODA, including mobilising other resources for sustainable development

The Czech Republic's bilateral and multilateral co-operation strategies recognise the need to raise development finance other than ODA (MFA, 2010; 2013). They also highlight the role that ODA can play in encouraging domestic reform in developing countries and in mobilising other resources for sustainable development.

While the Czech Republic does not have a specific policy for mobilising other resources for development, it supports domestic resource mobilisation in developing countries. For example, the Ministry of Finance provides technical assistance for public finance management, taxes and customs. The Czech Republic also promotes aid for trade to improve developing countries' trade performance and integration into the world economy. In 2014, it committed USD 7.4 million (16.2% of its bilateral ODA) to trade-related activities. It has also pledged USD 5.3 million to the Green Climate Fund (OECD, 2016).

The Czech Republic is starting to develop instruments for leveraging private sector investment for development. The MFA and the Czech Development Agency (CzDA) jointly support the Business Platform for Development Cooperation, which includes representatives of Czech private sector organisations. Its objective is to motivate Czech businesses to get involved in development co-operation, to respect corporate social responsibility principles and to develop inclusive business models that offer the potential for both commercial success and development impact.

New instruments to engage the private sector in development co-operation will need to be monitored

The Agency launched two instruments in 2013-14. These are: 1) the Development Partnership for the Private Sector Programme, which aims to facilitate business to business partnerships between Czech and developing country companies; and 2) the Feasibility Study Programme, which aims to co-finance costs for feasibility studies that analyse opportunities for economic projects with a development objective. Since these instruments are new, there is no evidence of how effective they are in mobilising private sector investment.

The Czech private sector has the potential to support sustainable investments for delivering the 2030 Agenda, including sharing expertise. However, the Czech Republic lacks an overall strategy for mobilising private sector resources for development, as well as a clear vision for how to support private sector development in developing countries. Instruments and activities are still seen as ways to help Czech businesses to succeed in national and international tenders for development projects, rather than as ways to encourage the Czech private sector to contribute to development in partner countries or territories through their own investments.

Awareness is low among businesses of how they could engage in development co-operation as a partner as opposed to benefitting from tied aid contracts (Chapter 5). The Business Platform for Development could put more emphasis on changing mind-sets about tied aid and raising awareness about other roles the private sector can play. At the same time, the Ministry of Foreign Affairs and the CzDA will need to find suitable expertise to identify opportunities to partner with private companies, to track development impact, and to manage conflicting objectives, if they arise.

Other flows are reported

Since 2014, the Czech Republic has been reporting other official finance (USD 5 million in 2014) and private flows (-111.45) to the OECD's Creditor Reporting System (CRS).

Notes

1. More information about the statements delivered by the Czech Republic during the inter-governmental negotiations for the 2030 Agenda available at www.iisd.ca/vol32/enb3215e.html and http://sd.iisd.org/news/un-general-debate-continues-addressing-post-2015-agenda-on-day-4/.

2. The "Housing in Liveable Cities" conference is an official part of preparations for the third global UN Conference on Housing and Sustainable Urban Development "Habitat III" that will be held in Ecuador in October 2016 prepared by the UN Human Settlements Programme (UN-Habitat). Its official outcome was the Prague Declaration. More information available at www.europeanhabitat.com/2016/03/21/the-czech-republic-greatly-managed-the-un-summit-on-sustainable-development/?lang=en.

3. During the inter-governmental negotiations for the adoption of the 2030 Agenda, the Czech Republic highlighted the importance of data collection and of monitoring and measuring progress using indicators that are precise, easy to communicate, and developed in sufficient time to ensure the identification of any potential pitfalls. More information available at www.iisd.ca/vol32/enb3216e.html and https://sustainabledevelopment.un.org/content/documents/13637czech.pdf.

4. The Commitment to Development Index (CDI), published annually by the Center for Global Development, ranks the world's richest countries according to the development-friendliness of their policies. More information at www.cgdev.org/cdi-2015.

5. More information about the Commitment to Development Index's score for the Czech Republic available at www.cgdev.org/cdi-2015/country/CZE.

6. These include: 1) the inter-ministerial preparatory consultations for the meetings of the government, where each proposal to be submitted to the government is discussed; 2) the Committee for the European Union, which is a government working body to consolidate Czech positions in the EU; and 3) the Council for Development Co-operation, an inter-ministerial coordinating body chaired by the Deputy Minister of Foreign Affairs responsible for development policy. The council's board members include representatives of all relevant ministries, the Office of the Government, and the Czech Statistical Office. Observers include the Czech Development Agency, the Czech NGO Forum for Development Co-operation, the Business Platform for Development Co-operation, the Association of Regions of the Czech Republic and the Union of Towns and Municipalities of the Czech Republic. 4) The Council of the Government for Sustainable Development, re-established in 2014, which is an advisory body to the government chaired by the Prime Minister. It has eight committees acting as consulting and peer review platforms.

7. CONCORD's 2015 spotlight report *Operationalising Policy Coherence for Development* places the parliaments of the Czech Republic in the category of critically low awareness of PCD (CONCORD, 2015).

Bibliography

Government sources

Council of Development Cooperation (2008), *Statute of the Council for International Development Cooperation,* (in Czech), Ministry of Foreign Affairs, Prague, www.mzv.cz/jnp/cz/zahranicni_vztahy/rozvojova_spoluprace/koordinace_zrs/rada_pro_zahranicni_rozvojovou/role_rady_pro_zrs_a_jeji_statut.html.

GoCR (2010), *The Strategic Framework for Sustainable Development in the Czech Republic,* Government of the Czech Republic, Resolution No. 37, 11 January 2010, www.mzp.cz/en/czech_republic_strategy_sd.

MFA (2016), "OECD Development Assistance Committee peer review: memorandum of the Czech Republic", unpublished, Ministry of Foreign Affairs, Prague.

MFA (2015), *Concept of the Czech Republic's Foreign Policy,* Ministry of Foreign Affairs, Prague, www.mzv.cz/jnp/en/foreign_relations/policy_planning/concept_of_the_czech_republic_s_foreign.html.

MFA (2013), *The Multilateral Development Co-operation Strategy of the Czech Republic 2013-2017,* Ministry of Foreign Affairs, Prague, www.mzv.cz/jnp/en/foreign_relations/development_cooperation_and_humanitarian/multilateral_development_cooperation/the_multilateral_development_cooperation.html.

MFA (2010), *The Development Co-operation Strategy of the Czech Republic 2010-2017,* Ministry of Foreign Affairs, Prague, www.mzv.cz/jnp/en/foreign_relations/development_cooperation_and_humanitarian/development_cooperation_strategy_of_the.html.

Other sources

CONCORD (2015), Operationalising Policy Coherence for Development – A Perspective of Civil Society on Institutional Systems for PCD in EU Member States, Spotlight Report 2015 Policy Paper, http://library.concordeurope.org/record/1634/files/DEEEP-REPORT-2016-008.pdf.

Dostál, V. (2014), *From Integration to Differentiation: The Czech Republic in the European Union Ten Years On,* DGAPanalyse, N° 9 May 2014. https://dgap.org/en/article/getFullPDF/25440.

EC (2015a), *Policy Coherence for Development: 2015 EU Report,* Czech contribution to questionnaire, https://ec.europa.eu/europeaid/sites/devco/files/reply-czech-republic_en.pdf.

EC (2015b), *Policy Coherence for Development: 2015 EU Report,* Commission staff working document. http://ec.europa.eu/europeaid/sites/devco/files/policy-coherence-for-development-2015-eu-report_en.pdf.

Glopolis (2012), *Policy Coherence for Development and the Common Agricultural Policy* (in Czech), Glopolis, Prague, http://glopolis.org/en/articles/policy-coherence-development-and-common-agricultural-policy/.

OECD (2016), Development Co-operation Report 2016: The Sustainable Development Goals as Business Opportunities, OECD Publishing, Paris. DOI: http://dx.doi.org/10.1787/dcr-2016-en.

OECD (2015), *Czech Republic: Follow-up to the Phase 3 Report & Recommendations,* May 2015, www.oecd.org/daf/anti-bribery/Czech-Republic-Phase-3-Written-Follow-Up-Report-ENG.pdf.

OECD (2013), *Phase 3 Report on Implementing the OECD Anti-Bribery Convention in the Czech Republic,* March 2013, www.oecd.org/daf/anti-bribery/CzechRepublicphase3reportEN.pdf.

Transparency International (2015), *Exporting Corruption – Progress Report 2015: Assessing Enforcement of the OECD Convention on Combatting Foreign Bribery*, 2016, www.transparency.org/whatwedo/publication/exporting_corruption_progress_report_2015_assessing_enforcement_of_the_oecd.

Transparency International (2014), *Corruption Perceptions Index 2014,* www.transparency.org/cpi2014/in_detail.

UN (2015), "Transforming our World: the 2030 Agenda for Sustainable Development", United Nations Resolution A/RES/70/1, 25 September 2015, https://sustainabledevelopment.un.org/post2015/transformingourworld/publication.

Chapter 2: The Czech Republic's vision and policies for development co-operation

Policies, strategies and commitments

Indicator: A clear policy vision and solid strategies guide the programme

The Czech Republic has a clear, broadly owned policy vision and medium-term strategy for its development co-operation, which is also valued within the Czech foreign policy. The Ministry of Foreign Affairs has started to identify priorities for the next medium-term strategy. It should seize the opportunity provided by a favourable domestic context for sustainable development to: strengthen the development dimension of Czech foreign policy, including how it will capitalise further on its evolving transition experience; and to integrate development co-operation into national efforts to deliver Agenda 2030.

The framework for development co-operation provides a solid basis for sharpening development priorities and aligning with the Sustainable Development Goals

The Czech Republic's overall vision and objectives for development co-operation are outlined clearly in the 2010 Act on Development Cooperation and Humanitarian Aid (GoCR, 2010). The act states that development co-operation aims to "contribute to eradicating poverty in the context of sustainable development, [...] to economic and social development, environmental protection, and promoting democracy, human rights and good governance in developing countries". The Czech Republic states that its comparative advantage is in sharing its specific experience and skills in transitioning to a democratic, market economy (MFA, 2010).

Czech foreign policy puts an emphasis on development and promoting key features of its own transformation experience such as the rule of law, good governance and democracy. Supporting global prosperity and sustainable development; and human dignity and human rights are two of the five objectives of the 2015 concept on foreign policy (MFA, 2015). The next development co-operation strategy, which will be implemented from 2018, is being prepared by the Ministry of Foreign Affairs in co-operation with the Council for Development Cooperation. As it defines future priorities and objectives, the Ministry has an opportunity to elevate development co-operation as a key pillar of foreign policy. It should also demonstrate how it will capitalise on its comparative advantage of political, economic and social transformation – an experience which is evolving – to eradicate poverty in the context of sustainable development. Sharing knowledge and experience which is based on historic experience and which tends to be tacit in nature is difficult to transmit and not automatic.

The Ministry of Foreign Affairs is also well placed to leverage high level political commitment to Agenda 2030 to better position development co-operation within the domestic debate and institutional set-up on the Sustainable Development Goals (SDGs) (Box 1.1). Official development assistance is part of Agenda 2030 and development co-operation should be integrated into national efforts to deliver Agenda 2030.

The Council for Development Cooperation serves as a useful platform to agree on strategic priorities and consult with key stakeholders. By consulting with parliamentarians the

Ministry of Foreign Affairs can broaden political ownership of the strategy. The Czech Republic has an asset in the expertise and knowledge of its civil society, think tanks, universities and line ministries, which can be useful as it elaborates its new strategy for development co-operation and the sustainable development goals.

Approach to allocating bilateral and multilateral aid

Indicator: The rationale for allocating aid and other resources is clear and evidence-based

The Czech Republic has a clear rationale and criteria for choosing partner countries or territories and sectors based on its comparative advantage and commitment to also support least developed countries. However, it is a challenge to get the right balance between its limited resources and the broad range of geographic and thematic priorities in the current strategy. The Ministry of Foreign Affairs recognises the need to concentrate bilateral aid better and is planning to reduce the number of geographic and thematic priorities in the next development co-operation strategy. Multilateral allocations account for a high share of Czech ODA. The Ministry of Foreign Affairs is working strategically to increase the visibility of the Czech Republic's policies and priorities in the European Union and other international organisations.

The Czech Republic plans to focus bilateral ODA on fewer countries and themes where the Czech Republic can add value

The 2010-2017 Development Cooperation Strategy outlines the criteria and rationale for allocating bilateral aid to 14 countries in the regions of Western Balkans and Eastern Europe, in Africa and in Asia (MFA, 2010; Chapter 3). It prioritises five broad sectors and three cross-cutting themes that are in line with the overall vision outlined in the act (GoCR, 2010).[1] In each sector it strives to transfer its expertise in social transformation, institution building and consolidating reform to developing and transition countries. It seeks to meet commitments it signed up to internationally, notably for least developed countries. Official development assistance is also used to respond to new foreign policy and political imperatives, such as instability in the region (e.g. Ukraine) and the ongoing refugee crisis.

The challenge for the Czech Republic is to focus a relatively small bilateral aid budget on all these priorities without fragmenting the portfolio or diluting its impact (Chapter 3). The Ministry of Foreign Affairs is taking steps to address this challenge. In particular, the concept note for the next medium-term strategy suggests reducing the number of partner countries or territories to six: three middle income countries (Bosnia and Herzegovina, Georgia and Moldova) and three least developed countries (Cambodia, Ethiopia and Zambia).[2] It intends to have development co-operation programmes with these six priority countries or territories and it will no longer have an additional category of 'project' countries, which in the current strategy contribute to fragmentation.

At the same time, Czech ministries report that technical assistance programmes related to the transition experience are in high demand, although this form of assistance accounts for a small and seemingly decreasing share of ODA (Chapter 3). The Ministry of Finance's economic transformation programme, for example, is flooded with requests, including from the EU, United Nations Development Programme (UNDP), World Bank and from a range of countries which are not always Czech focus countries. These ministries would benefit from guidance for providing technical assistance in priority and non-priority countries or territories.

Within its partner countries or territories the Czech Republic plans to focus on fewer themes and sectors – those where it can add value and maximise synergies among investments to increase sustainability. In addition, the Czech Development Agency and ministries managing transformation programmes[3] would need to narrow the scope of the interventions they support for greater impact and to reinforce coherence between the Czech development co-operation activities. The Ministry of Foreign Affairs could provide clearer guidelines for working in themes and sectors in a way that favours greater impact and supports partners efforts to achieve the SDGs.

The Czech Republic is well placed to strengthen its approach to multilateral co-operation and gain more policy influence

The overall goal of the Czech Republic's 2013-2017 Multilateral Development Cooperation Strategy is to maximise its support and contributions to multilateral organisations (MFA, 2013). Its four strategic goals are to: (1) promote the foreign and development policy priorities of the Czech Republic and contribute towards the global goals of development co-operation; (2) increase the influence and visibility of the Czech Republic through active involvement in decision-making processes; (3) help Czech entities with relevant expertise and know-how to win multilateral contracts; and (4) provide Czech expertise within international organisations.

As outlined in Chapter 1, the Czech Republic values the standard-setting and co-ordinating role of the multilateral system for achieving human rights, good governance and gender equality (MFA, 2013). Through its financial contributions to the European Union, it plays its part in supporting the EU as a leading provider of development assistance.

With about 70% of Czech ODA being channelled through the EU, UN agencies and the World Bank Group the government is under pressure to demonstrate what the Czech Republic gains directly from its multilateral investments (Chapter 3; Annex A). There is an explicit focus on winning contracts for Czech companies. A risk with this focus is that it does not necessarily match the reality of most Czech companies' capacity or interest in winning multilateral contracts (MFA, 2015). In addition, the administration risks investing limited capacity in this priority at the expense of others, such as finding synergies between multilateral and bilateral co-operation, shaping and influencing the international agenda in line with its development policy priorities and leveraging its specific transformation experience in multilateral settings.

While the Czech Republic has several good examples to build on (Box 2.1), there is scope to strengthen its leadership on issues that need to be advanced at the global and local level (e.g. governance, institution building). As the mid-term review of the multilateral strategy found, it is important to be realistic and strategic about what can be achieved and to have capable permanent representations in place (MFA, 2015; Chapter 7). Aware of this, the Czech Republic has strengthened capacity to engage in development issues in Brussels. Synergies and learning could also be enhanced through more systematic inter-ministerial co-ordination in relation to UN agencies and international financial institutions.

Box 2.1. The Czech Republic's contributions to multilateral organisations: good examples on which to build

The Czech Republic works with multilateral organisations to advance its priorities in several ways. For example:

- The Czech-UNDP Trust Fund, hosted by the UNDP Istanbul Centre, is proving to be successful in sharing Czech transition experience in Europe and Central Asia.
- Within the EU's *Agenda for Change*, the Czech Republic succeeded in including the following reference to transition experience: "building on the EU's own experience in managing transition" (EC, 2011).
- The World Bank and the Ministry of Finance work closely on capacity-building programmes in partner countries for transitioning to a market economy.
- The Ministry of the Environment and Ministry of Foreign Affairs played an active role in ensuring that the Third UN World Conference on Disaster Risk Reduction in 2015 in Sendai, Japan included specific indicators on resilience.

Source: Interviews by the peer review team in Prague.

Policy focus

Indicator: Fighting poverty, especially in least developed countries and fragile states, is prioritised

The Czech Republic adapts its development co-operation to different contexts, notably middle-income countries in the Western Balkans and Eastern Europe, and least developed countries. Although it targets vulnerability and inequalities in different contexts, it does not have a clear strategy or guidance for tackling poverty and focusing development co-operation where it is needed most while also being a niche provider, sharing its transformation experience. Clearer guidance and political leadership could help mainstream cross-cutting priorities into programmes and policy dialogue.

The Czech commitment to reducing poverty would be bolstered by guidance

The 2010 Act on Development Cooperation and Humanitarian Assistance commits the Czech Republic to fighting poverty in the context of sustainable development (GoCR, 2010). This commitment is also reflected in its priority sectors for support – essentially the social sectors, agriculture, and good governance – where progress can benefit poor and vulnerable people.

In Moldova and Ethiopia, for example, Czech projects target issues affecting vulnerable people, such as social protection for children of migrants in Moldova, and water and sanitation in the Southern Nations, Nationalities, and Peoples' Region (SNNPR) in Ethiopia (Annex C). However, it is hard to say how systematically the Czech Republic focuses on poverty reduction: it has yet to provide guidance, which would also provide a baseline for monitoring, on how to deliver this objective.

The Czech Republic is planning to shift the balance of aid programming with a view to allocating 50% of bilateral ODA to least developed countries (LDCs) by 2025. This is in line with international commitments to reverse the decline in ODA to LDCs. However, it is not clear how the Czech Republic will capitalise on its evolving transition experience in least developed countries. At present, this experience seems to be considered more relevant for transition countries in the neighbourhood than for developing countries. As it scales up its focus in the least developed countries, the Czech Republic will need to identify and explain how this support will add value and target poverty reduction.

There is awareness of the need for holistic responses between development and humanitarian programmes

The Czech Republic's overall strategy for development co-operation includes a chapter on humanitarian aid. Its memorandum to the Development Assistance Committee (DAC) also refers to efforts to create synergies between development and humanitarian programmes and improving links between relief and development, which it has been doing in Afghanistan, Ethiopia and the West Bank and Gaza Strip (MFA, 2016). However, the Czech Republic is not sufficiently equipped, in terms of scale of resources and instruments, to enable holistic responses between the two programmes (Chapter 7).

There is scope to specify how the Czech Republic will address fragility in its programmes

The Czech Republic actively supports international peacebuilding efforts and some of its current partner countries or territories are considered to be fragile (e.g. Afghanistan, Ethiopia, West Bank and Gaza Strip, Ukraine). While engaging in fragile states and situations is not a stated priority for the Czech Republic, it aligns with the European Union's orientations on fragility and has signed up to the Busan Partnership for Effective Development Co-operation, which includes commitments to address fragility (OECD, 2011).

Since the Czech Republic continues to work in states experiencing fragility, including from climate change, it should consider outlining how it will address this dimension in its policy dialogue and programming. At the same time, it should continue to be realistic and pragmatic about what it can achieve.

Guidance is needed to make progress on cross-cutting priorities

The Czech Republic's three cross-cutting priorities, as outlined in the 2010-2017 strategy, are (1) good (democratic) governance; (2) respect for the environment and the climate; and (3) respect for the basic human, economic, social and labour rights of beneficiaries, including gender equality. These issues, which are key goals of Agenda 2030 and the SDGs, are cross-cutting because they are relevant to all aspects of development.

Like other DAC members, the Czech Republic seeks to promote these priorities by mainstreaming them into all projects, as well as by supporting specific projects aimed at empowering women, improving central government, and climate change mitigation and adaptation. However, translating cross-cutting priorities into practice is a challenge for a range of reasons, as outlined in the DAC's "Lessons for Mainstreaming Cross-Cutting Issues" (OECD, 2014). Sustained political leadership, clear implementation guidelines with follow-up tools and practices, as well as sufficient financial and human resources are some of the keys to success.

Promoting and integrating cross-cutting priorities into the programme is still a work in progress. The Czech Development Agency (CzDA) needs clearer strategic guidance on what it should be aiming to achieve by mainstreaming these priorities, as recommended by the mid-term review of the 2010-2017 Development Co-operation Strategy. The Agency has focal points on environment and gender, who also deliver other tasks. It screens and monitors projects for the gender and environment focus and is trying to develop a methodology for integrating cross-cutting priorities into projects more systematically, specifically for gender equality. However, human resource capacity is constrained (chapter 4) and there is limited leadership and advocacy for these issues within the system.

Notes

1. The Czech Republic prioritises several sectors in the 2010-17 strategy. These include environment; agriculture; education, social and health services; economic development including energy and promoting democracy, human rights and social transformation.

2. Having exit strategies in place, as it does for Yemen, Viet Nam, Angola and Mongolia, can help ensure that successful projects remain sustainable and that partner governments are aware of Czech plans. It will also need to ensure that it invests more bilateral aid in fewer and larger programmes in the priority countries or territories.

3. Two of the most established transformation programmes are the "Transformation Cooperation Programme" managed by the Department of Human Rights and Transition Policy at the Ministry of Foreign Affairs and the "Financial and Economic Transformation" technical co-operation programme of the Ministry of Finance.

Bibliography

Government sources

GoCR (2010), *Act on Development Cooperation and Humanitarian Aid, and Amending Related Laws*, Government of the Czech Republic, Prague.

MFA (2016), "OECD Development Assistance Committee peer review: memorandum of the Czech Republic", unpublished, Ministry of Foreign Affairs, Prague.

MFA (2015), *Concept of the Czech Republic's Foreign Policy*, Policy Planning Department, Ministry of Foreign Affairs, Prague.

MFA (2014), *Medium-term Evaluation of the 2010-2017 Concept of International Development Cooperation of the Czech Republic*, translated from the Czech language into English by the Czech Authorities, Ministry of Foreign Affairs, Prague.

MFA (2013), *The Multilateral Development Cooperation Strategy of the Czech Republic 2013-2017*, Ministry of Foreign Affairs, Prague, www.mzv.cz/jnp/en/foreign_relations/development_cooperation_and_humanitarian/multilateral_development_cooperation/the_multilateral_development_cooperation.html.

MFA (2010), *The Development Cooperation Strategy of the Czech Republic 2010-2017*, Ministry of Foreign Affairs, Prague, www.mzv.cz/jnp/en/foreign_relations/development_cooperation_and_humanitarian/development_cooperation_strategy_of_the.html.

Other sources and references

Czech Forum for Development Co-operation (2015), *Executive Summary of the Czech Aidwatch report 2015*, FoRS, Prague www.fors.cz/wp-content/uploads/2012/08/Aidwatch-2015.pdf.

EC (2011), *Increasing the Impact of EU Development Policy: An Agenda for Change*, Communication from the Commission to the European Parliament, the Council, the European Economic and Social Committee and the Committee of the Regions, European Commission, Brussels, http://eur-lex.europa.eu/legal-content/EN/TXT/PDF/?uri=CELEX%3A52011DC0637&qid=1412922281378&from=EN.

OECD (2014), *Mainstreaming Cross-cutting Issues: 7 lessons from DAC peer reviews*, OECD, Paris, www.oecd.org/dac/peer-reviews/Final%20publication%20version%20of%20the%207%20Lessons%20mainstreaming%20cross%20cutting%20issues.pdf.

OECD (2011),"Busan Partnership for Effective Development Co-operation", Fourth High Level Forum on Aid Effectiveness, Busan, Republic of Korea, 29 November-1 December 2011, www.oecd.org/dac/effectiveness/49650173.pdf.

Chapter 3: Allocating the Czech Republic's official development assistance

Overall ODA volume

Indicator: The member makes every effort to meet ODA domestic and international targets

The Czech Republic has reiterated its commitment to the target of allocating 0.33% of its gross national income (GNI) as ODA by 2030. Although the Ministry of Foreign Affairs has prepared a timeline with annual milestones to grow the ODA budget from 0.12% of GNI in 2015 to 0.17% by 2020, a more ambitious plan will be needed if it wants to be credible about reaching its 0.33% commitment. The Czech Republic's statistical reporting on its ODA allocations is timely and conforms to OECD guidelines.

The Czech Republic will need to scale up to achieve its ODA/GNI target of 0.33% by 2030

The Czech Republic's net ODA increased by 11.4% in real terms in 2015, according to preliminary data, to reach USD 236 million (up from USD 212 million in 2014).[1] Its ODA/GNI ratio rose to 0.12% from 0.11% in 2014 (OECD, 2016). The Czech Republic re-committed to provide 0.33% of GNI as ODA by 2030 at the Third International Conference on Financing for Development, held in Addis Ababa in 2015. To meet this target, it will need to increase the ODA budget significantly.

A key feature of Czech ODA is the high share of the total (71%) that is allocated to multilateral organisations (Figure 3.1). This is the result of the high amount of assessed contributions that the Czech Republic allocates to multilateral organisations – mainly the EU – compared to its small bilateral ODA budget.

The increase in total ODA in 2015 was mostly in the bilateral budget, which is in line with plans to scale up bilateral aid. It also reverses a declining trend, which saw bilateral aid decrease by about USD 41 million between 2009 and 2013 (in 2014 constant prices) (Figure 3.1). Development Assistance Committee (DAC) statistics show that the biggest cut in bilateral allocations over this period was in the provision of experts and technical assistance (from USD 23 million in 2010 to USD 6 million in 2014) and in aid to Central Asia (see Annex A, Tables A.2 and A.3). Allocations to Central Asia declined in line with phasing-out of the Provincial Reconstruction Team in Logar, Afghanistan.

The time is ripe to scale up ODA and raise the Czech Republic's donor profile

The Czech Republic plans to grow the ODA budget to reach 0.17% of GNI by 2020 – its incremental plan aims for an annual increase of CZK 200 million (approximately USD 8 million[2]), with an emphasis on increasing bilateral allocations. The MFA states that it plans to double its bilateral allocations to the Czech Development Agency (from CZK 483 million in 2015 to CZK 883 million – approximately USD 40 million - in 2020), while also increasing humanitarian aid. These projected increases are heading in the right direction. However, to meet its 0.33% target by 2030, the Czech Republic will need a more ambitious growth plan. The Czech Republic is recovering well from the financial crisis[3] and the government is moving towards a budget surplus. The time is ripe to scale up the bilateral programme and to raise the country's profile as a donor, building on its already well-functioning bilateral co-operation system.

Figure 3.1 Trends in the Czech Republic's ODA flows, 2004-2014

USD million, constant prices (USD 2014)

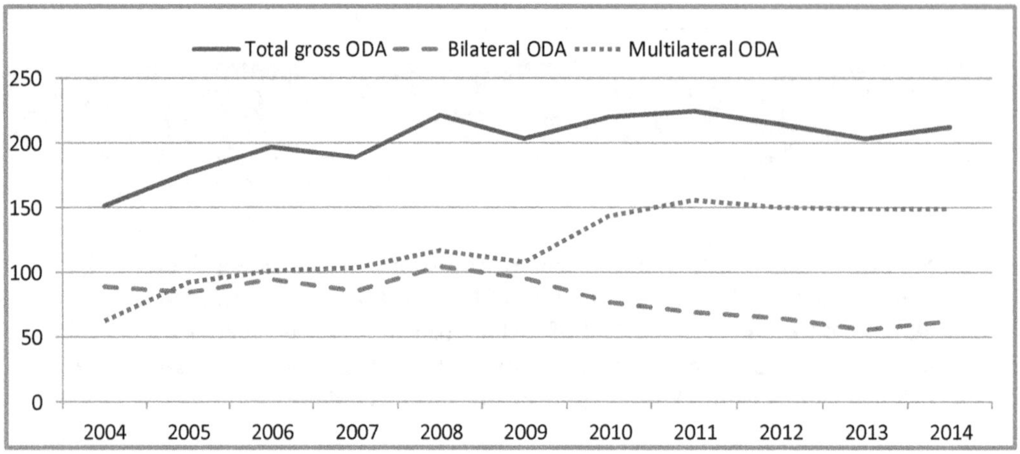

Source: OECD (2016), "Detailed aid statistics: Official and private flows", OECD International Development Statistics (database), DOI: http://dx.doi.org/10.1787/data-00072-en (Accessed on 05 July 2016)

The Czech Republic's ODA reporting conforms to OECD rules

Since joining the DAC in 2013, the Czech Republic has significantly improved its statistical reporting to the DAC Creditor Reporting System. The reporting conforms to DAC ODA rules. The Czech Republic is also in line with the DAC Recommendation on Terms and Conditions of Aid. Its development assistance is delivered exclusively in the form of grant aid. However, a high share (67.6%) of bilateral ODA is tied (Annex A, Table A.6 and Chapter 5).

The Czech Republic ensures at least three years predictability of its future country and sector aid flows. In its response to the 2016 DAC Survey on Donors' Forward Spending Plans, the Czech Republic provided an outlook of its bilateral allocations up to 2019 (OECD, forthcoming). All allocations for priority partner countries or territories – structured by priority sectors – are indicated in Czech crowns in the annual Development Cooperation Plan,[4] which includes the budget for the coming year and an indicative outlook for another two years (Chapter 5).

Bilateral ODA allocations

Indicator: Aid is allocated according to the statement of intent and international commitments

The Czech Republic allocates its bilateral aid according to its geographical and sectoral priorities. However, the high number of activities implemented within countries and territories results in a fragmented aid portfolio. Reducing the number of priority countries or territories and moving from a package of small, stand-alone projects to more integrated programming and thematic approaches would ensure greater efficiency and impact.

The Czech Republic's priority countries or territories receive a high share of bilateral aid

In 2014, 29.5% of the Czech Republic's total ODA was provided bilaterally, amounting to USD 62.6 million (OECD, 2016). According to its memorandum to the DAC, the Czech Republic now has 11 priority partner countries or territories, instead of 14 mentioned in the 2010-2017 Development Cooperation Strategy.[5] It engages in programme co-operation with five of these – Afghanistan, Bosnia and Herzegovina, Ethiopia, Moldova and Mongolia – and has projects in the other six – Cambodia, Georgia, Kosovo, Serbia, the West Bank and Gaza Strip, and Zambia. Overall, ODA allocations reflect the geographical priorities: in 2013-14 its 11 priority countries or territories received 48% of gross bilateral aid (Figure 3.3) and eight of them were among its top 10 ODA recipients (Annex A). The Czech Republic allocated over half of its bilateral aid to its top 10 recipients (56%) in 2013-14, compared to the DAC average of 36% (Annex A).

The highest share (52%) of Czech gross bilateral aid went to lower-middle income countries in 2014, reflecting its strategic focus on countries in the Western Balkans and Eastern Europe. In addition, it allocated 27% of its bilateral ODA to least developed countries (LDCs); one percent more than in 2013 (26%). Total ODA to LDCs equalled 0.03% of Czech GNI in 2014. According to its memorandum, the Czech Republic plans to increase the share of ODA going to LDCs to contribute to achieving the EU collective target of 0.15% to 0.20% of GNI in the short term and 0.20% within the frame of the 2030 Agenda (MFA, 2016; Chapter 2).

In line with its plans to concentrate its aid further, the Czech Republic intends to reduce the number of priority countries or territories from 11 to 6 – Bosnia-Herzegovina, Cambodia, Ethiopia, Georgia, Moldova, and Zambia – three of which are LDCs (Chapter 2). By reducing the number of priority countries or territories, it will be in a position to increase the budget envelope for these countries and, if it manages allocations strategically, it can increase the scale of its projects and programmes for greater impact, as requested by partners in Ethiopia and Moldova (Annex C).

Figure 3.2 The Czech Republic's bilateral ODA to priority countries or territories

2013-14 average, gross disbursements

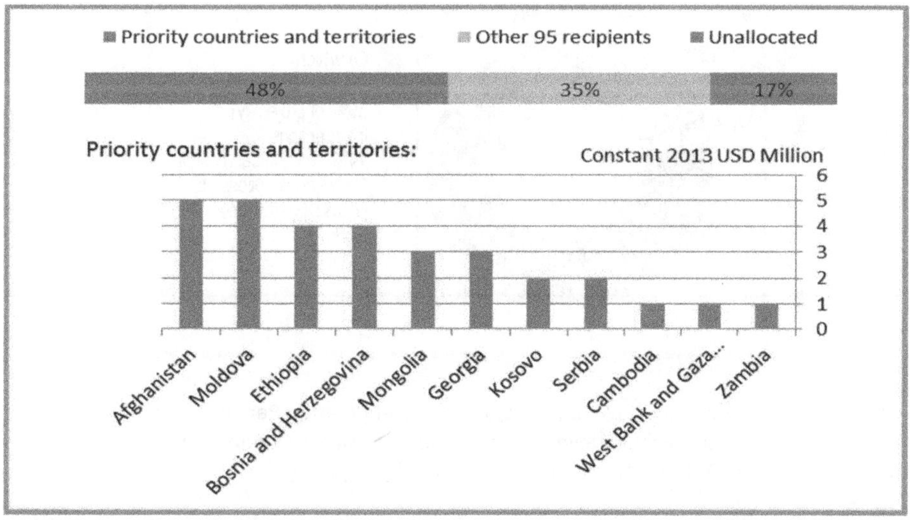

Source: OECD (2016), "Geographical distribution of financial flows: Flows to developing countries", OECD International Development Statistics (database).DOI: http://dx.doi.org/10.1787/data-00566-en (Accessed on 05 July 2016)

Overall sector allocations reflect strategic priorities, but aid in partner countries or territories is dispersed

The Czech Republic has a broad set of sectoral priorities, which are specified in its Development Cooperation Strategy 2010-2017. It ensures that allocations are aligned with these priorities by dedicating specific budget lines to each sector in its annual Development Cooperation Plan. In 2013-14, Czech bilateral aid focused mostly on education (17% of gross bilateral aid), government and civil society (13%, decreasing from 28% in 2008-12), water supply and sanitation and agriculture (receiving 8% of gross bilateral aid each). In-donor refugee costs and humanitarian aid received 18% and 10% of gross bilateral aid respectively in 2013-14 (Table A.5, Annex A).

Gender equality and environment are two of the cross-cutting priority themes of Czech development co-operation (MZV ČR, 2010; Chapter 2). In 2014, 19.9% of Czech bilateral allocable aid had gender equality and women's empowerment as a principal or significant objective, which is lower than the DAC average of 34.7% (OECD, 2016) and lower than could be expected given Czech investments in education, for example. Czech support to the environment has been increasing in recent years, both in terms of volume and as a share of bilateral allocable aid, reaching 21.1% in 2014. However, it is still lower than the DAC average of 32.2%. The Czech share of bilateral allocable aid focusing specifically on climate change reached 11.9% in 2014, well below the DAC average of 23.9% (OECD, 2016).

Figure 3.3 Composition of the Czech Republic's bilateral ODA, 2014

Gross disbursements

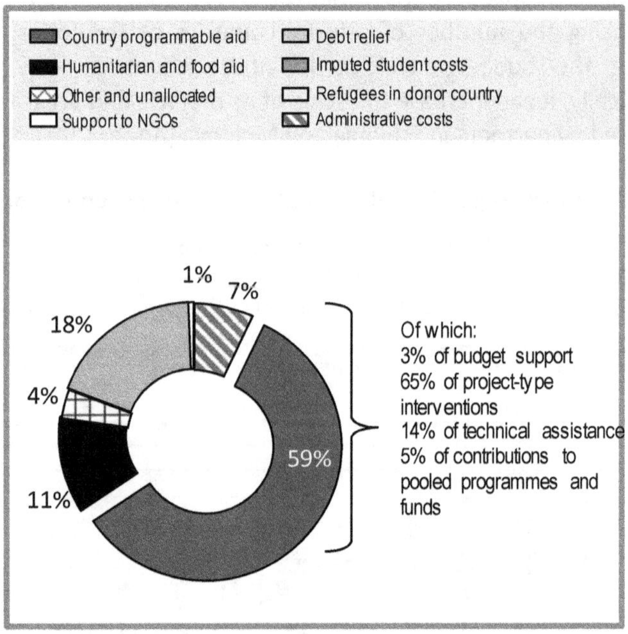

Country programmable aid
Humanitarian and food aid
Other and unallocated
Support to NGOs
Debt relief
Imputed student costs
Refugees in donor country
Administrative costs

1%
7%
18%
4%
11%
59%

Of which:
3% of budget support
65% of project-type interventions
14% of technical assistance
5% of contributions to pooled programmes and funds

Source: OECD (2016), Development Co-operation Report 2016: The Sustainable Development Goals as Business Opportunities, OECD Publishing, Paris. DOI: http://dx.doi.org/10.1787/dcr-2016-en

In 2014, the Czech Republic programmed 58.5% of its bilateral ODA at partner country or territory level (OECD, 2016). Figure 3.3 shows that the biggest share (65%) of its country programmable aid (CPA) was made up of project-type interventions, followed by technical assistance (14%).

In priority countries or territories, the various institutions that make up the Czech co-operation system implement a large number of activities across a broad spectrum of sectors.[6] The result is a fragmented portfolio. Table 3.1 shows how Czech CPA is dispersed around a high number of sectors and activities in programme countries. It is difficult to have an impact on development when an already limited country budget is allocated to so many small activities – often stand-alone projects - in different sectors. Moreover, this fragmentation results in high administrative costs in setting up and following up on the many activities. The Czech Republic is planning to reduce the number of sectors in priority countries or territories to not more than three, in line with EU directives, and to move from project-level activities to a more thematic and programmatic approach.[7] It can also ensure greater impact by concentrating aid and focusing it on themes where it has specific expertise and by maximising synergies between different activities.[8]

Table 3.1 Number of Czech country programmable aid activities in its programme countries, 2014

Programme countries	Total CPA (2013 USD million)	Number of CPA activities reported in the CRS[9]	Number of sectors in which CPA activities are reported
Afghanistan	5.9	20	8
Bosnia-Herzegovina	3.5	65	10
Ethiopia	3.2	30	5
Moldova	5.1	42	8
Mongolia	2.6	17	9

Source: OECD (2016), "Creditor Reporting System: Aid activities", OECD International Development Statistics (database), DOI: http://dx.doi.org/10.1787/data-00061-en (Accessed on 05 July 2016)

Multilateral ODA channel

Indicator: The member uses the multilateral aid channels effectively

The Czech Republic's core multilateral ODA mainly fulfils its mandatory assessed contributions to the EU and other international organisations. Earmarked contributions are low and directed strategically to UN agencies that are eager to work with small donors and whose objectives align with Czech interests and priorities, notably making use of its transition expertise and experience.

ODA to multilateral agencies is mainly driven by legally binding agreements

Multilateral ODA represents the most important share of Czech ODA – a share that has been increasing in recent years (Figure 3.1). In 2014, the Czech Republic's total funding of the multilateral system amounted to 71.9% of total gross ODA: 70.5% mandatory and voluntary core contributions and 1.4% earmarked/multi-bi contributions. While the Czech Republic channels most of its multilateral ODA through the EU (85% in 2014), it also contributes to the United Nations and other multilateral organisations (Annex A, tables 2 and 6).

Earmarked contributions are very marginal and mainly channelled through trust funds. This support is either used to promote the use of Czech expertise in certain areas – such as its transition experience in Eastern Europe and Central Asia through the United Nations Development Programme (UNDP) Istanbul Centre – or to support objectives that the Czech Republic would not be able to pursue as a small bilateral donor such as through UNDP's Funding Facility for Immediate Stabilization in Iraq. In line with good practice, the Czech Republic tries to align with the priorities of the multilateral organisations and avoid adding to the administrative burden, as confirmed by multilateral partners.

Notes

1. Amounts are in USD 2014 constant prices. In 2015 current prices, Czech net ODA amounted to USD 202 million in 2015.
2. Using 2015 exchange rate of 1 USD = CZK 24.5926.
3. The OECD's economic forecast summary for the Czech Republic can be found at www.oecd.org/eco/outlook/czech-republic-economic-forecast-summary.htm. Information on its general government budget can be found at www.oecd.org/gov/Czech-Republic.pdf and https://data.oecd.org/gga/general-government-deficit.htm#indicator-chart.
4. Czech Development Cooperation Plans from 2011 to 2016 can be found at www.mzv.cz/jnp/en/foreign_relations/development_cooperation_and_humanitarian/information_statistics_publications/czech_development_cooperation_plan_for.html.
5. The Development Cooperation Strategy 2010-17 (MFA, 2010) listed 14 priority countries or territories split into three groups: 1) five priority countries or territories with a co-operation programme (Afghanistan, Bosnia and Herzegovina, Ethiopia, Moldova and Mongolia); 2) five priority countries or territories without a co-operation programme but benefitting from co-operation projects (Georgia, Cambodia, Kosovo, Serbia and the West Bank and Gaza Strip) and; 3) four phasing out countries (Angola, Yemen, Viet Nam, and Zambia). Bilateral co-operation activities were terminated in 2015 in Angola, Viet Nam and Yemen after a mid-term review of the 2010-2017 Development Co-operation Strategy. In its memorandum for the peer review, the Czech Republic indicates that it focuses on only 11 priority countries or territories – those indicated in points 1) and 2) above and Zambia (MFA, 2016).
6. For instance, as indicated in its memorandum to the DAC (MFA, 2016), in 2014 the CzDA implemented 123 projects for a total budget of USD 17.6 million and Czech embassies implemented 157 local small projects in 53 countries and 14 projects with the Business Development Partnership in 9 countries.
7. At the same time, embassies are receiving instructions from Prague to increase the minimum size of small-scale projects.
8. This was also suggested by evaluations of Czech official development co-operation, such as those of the water and sanitation sector in Ethiopia and Moldova. See www.mzv.cz/file/1314382/Ethiopia_Evaluation_text_2014.pdf and www.mzv.cz/file/1740448/Summary_evaluation_water_and_sanitation_MD_EN.pdf.
9. The number of activities reported includes entries reported in the DAC CRS database for: contributions to specific-purpose programmes and funds managed by international organisations; other technical assistance; project-type interventions; and sector budget support.

Bibliography

Government sources

MFA (2016), "OECD Development Assistance Committee peer review: memorandum of the Czech Republic", unpublished, Ministry of Foreign Affairs, Prague.

MFA (2013), *The Multilateral Development Cooperation Strategy of the Czech Republic 2013-2017*, Ministry of Foreign Affairs, Prague, www.mzv.cz/jnp/en/foreign_relations/development_cooperation_and_humanitarian/multilateral_development_cooperation/the_multilateral_development_cooperation.html.

MFA (2010), *The Development Cooperation Strategy of the Czech Republic 2010-2017,* Ministry of Foreign Affairs, Prague, www.mzv.cz/jnp/en/foreign_relations/development_cooperation_and_humanitarian/development_cooperation_strategy_of_the.html.

Other sources

OECD (2016), Development Co-operation Report 2016: The Sustainable Development Goals as Business Opportunities, OECD Publishing, Paris. DOI: http://dx.doi.org/10.1787/dcr-2016-en.

OECD (2014), *Global Outlook on Aid - Results of the 2014 DAC Survey on Donors' Forward Spending Plans and Prospects for Improving Aid Predictability,* OECD, Paris, www.oecd.org/dac/aid-architecture/GlobalOutlookAid-web.pdf.

OECD (forthcoming), 2016 Global Outlook on Aid: Results of the 2016 DAC Survey on Donors' Spending Plans and Prospects for Improving Aid Predictability, OECD Publishing, Paris.

Chapter 4: Managing the Czech Republic's development co-operation

Institutional system

Indicator: The institutional structure is conducive to consistent, quality development co-operation

The Czech Republic has a sound institutional structure and system for development co-operation. It has built up several assets, including political and strategic leadership at the Ministry of Foreign Affairs; an inter-ministerial Council for Development Cooperation for exchanging information and building cross-government ownership of the programme; and the Czech Development Agency, which is recognised as a capable implementing body. Nevertheless, while the institutional system is conducive to quality development co-operation, the system is also vulnerable due to capacity and resource constraints. A more systematic whole of government approach that promotes synergies among Czech activities could reinforce the impact of development co-operation in partner countries or territories.

The institutional set-up is sound and led by the Ministry of Foreign Affairs

Over the past decade, following a major reform in 2007, the Czech Republic has put in place a sound system for managing development co-operation (see Annex B). This was confirmed by the Supreme Audit Office in 2015, whose audit found that the system functions well (Supreme Audit Office, 2015).

The Ministry of Foreign Affairs' mandate is clearly outlined in the 2010 Act on Development Cooperation and Humanitarian Aid: it should lead, co-ordinate and oversee the delivery of the Czech Republic's official development assistance (GoCR, 2010). Since 2010, the Ministry has consolidated its position as the institutional leader of the development co-operation system. A key success factor has been to streamline aid expenditures into one main budget line administered by the Ministry of Foreign Affairs.[1] With financial authority over the majority of the bilateral aid budget,[2] 50% of which is implemented by the Czech Development Agency (CzDA), the MFA is well-placed to steer aid planning and programming within the overall medium-term strategy and annual spending plans.

There seems to be cross-government ownership and awareness of Czech development co-operation

The Czech Republic has two main instruments which work well in co-ordinating development co-operation at headquarters. First, the inter-ministerial Council for Development Cooperation serves as an important forum for discussing and approving development strategies and plans, strengthening development practice through its working groups and getting cross-government buy-in.[3] The council helps to promote cross-government efforts to capitalise on the expertise of line ministries, non-governmental organisations (NGOs), the private sector and public authorities in managing transition reforms.[4]

Second, the annual plan for development co-operation is a whole-of-government expenditure plan with an indicative budget outlook for the following two years. This plan is discussed in the council and approved by the government (MFA, 2016a).

Czech ministries collaborate well in the event of natural disasters or on specific issues such as the current refugee crisis. In particular, the State Council on Foreign and Security Policy provides space for inter-ministerial discussion on political, development, humanitarian and security-related efforts in crisis-affected countries (e.g. Syria and Ukraine).

Limited time and staff available within ministries seem to be a challenge for managing and responding to demands from developing countries for transitional-related technical assistance, which is declining as a share of ODA (Chapters 2 and 3). The Czech Development Agency has started to play a facilitative role by finding and sending Czech experts from line ministries to partner country or territory institutions. It could perhaps also try to find other ways to increase efficiencies to maximise this support. The government would need, however, to have a clear vision and strategy for capitalising further on this technical assistance (Chapter 2).

There is scope to enhance whole-of-government co-ordination of Czech activities within partner countries or territories

The country strategy papers for programme countries which are prepared by the Ministry of Foreign Affairs include the activities supported by the MFA and the Agency. Some Czech line ministries have a limited number of projects in partner countries or territories – especially in the Western Balkans and Eastern Europe – but these are not necessarily included in the country programme or the memorandum of understanding between the Ministry of Foreign Affairs and the partner government. Evaluations of programmes in Moldova, Georgia and Ethiopia found that this was the case with aid-for-trade projects and some activities by the ministries of the environment and the interior.

There is potential for promoting greater synergies among all Czech actions in partner countries or territories through a more strategic, co-ordinated whole-of-government approach. Doing this could help increase the overall impact and visibility of Czech ODA in partner countries or territories. There is an opportunity to adopt this approach as the Czech Republic focuses its support on fewer priority countries or territories (Chapter 2 and 3), has a stronger field presence by decentralising project management by the Agency to the field, and prepares the second generation of country strategies.

There is scope to reinforce the Ministry of Foreign Affairs' capacity

The division of labour for managing development co-operation within the two principal institutions is clear on the strategic level: the Ministry of Foreign Affairs is responsible for policy making and for setting strategic priorities, while the Agency implements most of the bilateral development co-operation. As outlined in its memorandum, within the MFA, the Department of Development Cooperation and Humanitarian Assistance is responsible for a range of functions (MFA, 2016b). But its small staff size (just 13 staff in headquarters) prevents the department from strengthening the system further. The Ministry of Foreign Affairs is aware that there is still scope to reinforce the structure and adapt the systems to ensure that they remain fit for purpose in a rapidly changing global context for development co-operation and as partners' needs evolve.

While there is no delegation of authority to embassies in programme countries, since 2013 "development diplomats"[5] have been assigned to embassies in programme countries. These embassies also have a local project co-ordinator. The government is planning to step up its field presence through the Agency which will decentralise some operations to the country level.

The political leadership at the MFA is reviewing how to strengthen the department's capacity and core competencies for development co-operation. Stronger policy capacity would enable the MFA to advance a number of strategic priorities, including:

- Taking forward the development co-operation dimension of Agenda 2030, ensuring that development co-operation is anchored in the Czech SDG Action Plan, and maximising synergies across different policy areas at a time when Agenda 2030 requires more integrated and system-wide approaches.
- Reinforcing the division of responsibilities and roles between the Ministry of Foreign Affairs and the Agency, notably the Ministry's role in setting policy and preparing specific guidelines for implementing priorities (Chapter 2). The MFA should also set out clearly the roles and responsibilities for the embassy and the Agency in the field, including relations with headquarters.
- Continuing to raise the visibility of development co-operation as a key pillar of foreign policy, and providing adequate policy guidance to the CzDA (Chapter 2).

Adaptation to change

Indicator: The system is able to reform and innovate to meet evolving needs

The system for development co-operation has been transformed since 2007 and is capable of implementing the existing strategy. At the same time, current rules and procedures leave little room for the innovation and reform required for Czech development co-operation to adapt to a changing international context.

Significant organisational change at the Czech Development Agency has strengthened its capacity

The Czech Republic has continued to transform the Czech Development Agency into a capable implementing body. The Agency has evolved from two to four departments and staff numbers have grown; it has also strengthened its procedures, systems and approaches. Project management capacity has grown and the project cycle manual is a useful, solid and adaptable tool which helps ensure a systematic and transparent approach to project management (Chapter 5). The Agency has a clear strategic vision for the medium-term, prioritising more and better impact in partner countries or territories and strengthening its capacity to be ready for new challenges and priorities.

The return on this effort is greater confidence across the system in the Czech Development Agency's capacity to deliver aid, as shown by the positive findings of a recent audit (Supreme Audit Office, 2015). This gives greater legitimacy to proposals to increase ODA (Chapter 3) – as the Agency has the capacity to absorb a larger budget – and to decentralise staff to the field, starting with Ethiopia in 2016. Once in the field, the Agency will be better placed to identify country needs, to complement the embassy's role by freeing up time for development diplomats to engage more in policy dialogue, to reinforce project management and promote greater synergies among Czech activities and support by other donors (Annex C). To achieve these objectives, staff will need sufficient decision-making and financial authority, with appropriate strategic direction and guidance from headquarters.

Rule and procedures limit capacity to innovate

The Czech system is still developing and consolidating. Nevertheless, certain rigidities are built into the system, which limit flexibility. An example is the requirement to deliver grant projects through entities registered in the Czech Republic. The development co-operation system would benefit from greater flexibility so as (1) to deliver aid through a broader mix of mechanisms that are not tied to Czech entities; and (2) to innovate, take calculated risks and engage in multi-year partnerships and programmes (Chapter 5). The first step in overcoming these constraints will be to demonstrate to Czech decision makers and implementing partners which rules and procedures undermine the efficiency and effectiveness of Czech development co-operation.

Human resources

Indicator: The member manages its human resources effectively to respond to field imperatives

Having adequate human resource capacity within the Ministry of Foreign Affairs and the Czech Development Agency to deliver on core and emerging priorities is a challenge. The political leadership at the Ministry of Foreign Affairs and senior management within the Department for Development Cooperation are aware of the main human resources constraints and plan to address some of the constraints between 2016 and 2020 in line with increases in the aid budget. There is also scope for the Ministry of Foreign Affairs to place stronger emphasis on the specific needs of the development co-operation programme when rotating staff and through more tailor-made training.

Limited human resource capacity is a challenge for the system

Human resource management, notably having adequate staff and capacity, is a key vulnerability of the Czech development co-operation system. At the Ministry of Foreign Affairs, human resources are stretched with individual staff managing several large portfolios at once.[6] Capacity is very limited in certain areas (e.g. in statistics and evaluation) and bringing in professional expertise such as legal advice when specific needs arise is complex. Nevertheless, the Department for Development Co-operation and Humanitarian Assistance has had some success – through personal contacts and informal networks – in attracting Ministry staff interested in development to work in the department, rotate to embassies in partner countries or territories and in maintaining their engagement in the programme.

Strict rules on recruitment levels at the Czech Development Agency and a relatively low allowance for administrative costs (5% of admin costs for projects for staffing and expenses) also restrict its flexibility to manage human resources according to need. Nevertheless, capacity in the Agency has increased, with five new positions created in 2016 giving it 23 staff in all. The political leadership is planning to address some key staffing constraints by increasing staffing levels both at the Ministry and the Agency under the next development co-operation strategy (Table 4.1; MFA, 2016a). In this context, the Agency would benefit from greater capacity in legal issues, procurement, risk management, cross-cutting issues and quality control. Having adequate staffing levels is also central to the Agency delivering on its vision to decentralise and deploy more people to all priority countries or territories.

The Ministry of Foreign Affairs could consider taking additional measures to help ensure that human resources can respond effectively to the needs of the development co-operation programme. At present, its overall human resource policy does not make provisions for the specific human resource needs related to development co-operation. Like in other Development Assistance Committee (DAC) countries, where development co-operation is integrated into Ministry of Foreign Affairs, rotation of diplomats can pose challenges, especially in terms of losing key competencies when staff move to new positions. For example, while the Department tries to ensure that the "development diplomats" deployed by the Ministry to priority countries or territories have relevant experience and skills for delivering the development programme, this is not guaranteed and training is limited (see next section).

Embassies can now recruit local staff to support the development diplomats, especially in relation to project monitoring and relations with the partner government. While local staff cannot formally report to headquarters, some draft monitoring reports in Czech or English, which are then submitted by diplomats to headquarters (Annex C).

Table 4.1 Indicative plans for human resources at the Ministry of Foreign Affairs and the Agency

	Staffing default status in 2016	2017	2018	2019	2020
Ministry of Foreign Affairs	17	+3	+2	+2	+1
Czech Development Agency	23	+5	+4	+3	+3

Source: MFA A (2016a), Draft Concept Note: Implementation of bilateral international development co-operation after 2017, unpublished, unofficial translation from the Czech language into English (Google translate)

Development competencies and knowledge in the Ministry of Foreign Affairs could be boosted through tailored training

Training at the Ministry of Foreign Affairs should be strengthened in order to build up key development co-operation competencies. Formal training and programmes for skills development are limited although the Diplomatic Academy includes development as a topic in its curriculum for new diplomats. To raise awareness of the development co-operation priorities and programme, the MFA relies on awareness-raising sessions at the annual meeting of overseas staff and provides a lecture on development co-operation to diplomats heading overseas. There is also two weeks of training for development diplomats, which is provided by staff at the Department for Development Co-operation and Humanitarian Assistance and the Agency and some guidance is provided through the annual work plan.

However, given the specific (often technical) tasks demanded of generalist diplomats posted to embassies in priority countries or territories for development co-operation, the ministry should consider providing access to tailor-made training for these diplomats and local project co-ordinators. Specific issues for training could include project management, managing for results, managing risk, and the principles of effective development. There is also potential for greater experience-sharing among those embassies where the Czech Republic has a development co-operation programme, for example by creating a network of development diplomats.

The Agency is placing increasing emphasis on staff development through its training guidelines, mostly in languages and project cycle management. Staff training needs are discussed during annual performance reviews. A system of seconding staff to the Czech/ United Nations Development Programme (UNDP) Trust also helps build experience (Chapter 2).

Notes

1. Prior to 2007, the system and ODA budget were highly fragmented, involving actions by several ministries. It took the Czech Republic four years to prepare and approve the legal act (2010) and two years to get support to set up the Agency.

2. The Ministry of Finance also approves budgetary allocations from the Ministry of Foreign Affairs to line ministries.

3. The inter-ministerial council is chaired by the Deputy Minister of Foreign Affairs, and includes observers from civil society, the Czech Development Agency, municipalities and business. It has standing working groups on strategies, evaluation and global education and ad hoc working groups on ODA methodology and aid for trade.

4. Several ministries implement activities which are funded by the MFA budget (e.g. Ministry of Interior and Ministry of Industry and Trade) and a small share of bilateral ODA is funded from individual ministries' budgets. These activities are included in the annual plan for development co-operation (e.g. Ministry of Education scholarships). Technical assistance support is in high demand (e.g. Ministry of Finance and Ministry of the Environment).

5. The Czech Republic used the term "Development Diplomat" for a regular diplomat based in an embassy in a priority country or territory. His or her terms of reference include identifying and monitoring development projects and dialogue with the partner government. The development diplomats' roles and responsibilities are outlined in the project cycle management methodology (MFA, 2011) and in the annual guidelines and work plan.

6. For example, the Deputy Director of the whole department is also in charge of the humanitarian agenda which includes annual humanitarian planning and funding, organising the four annual calls for proposal, and supervising project implementation through partners or embassies, preparing reports and regularly liaising with the permanent representatives in Geneva, New York, Rome and Brussels. Development diplomats work part-time on development, yet they must deliver a broad range of tasks, including discussing development priorities with the partner government, identifying potential projects with the government, publicising the scholarship programme, managing the small grants scheme, co-ordinating with other providers, and monitoring the Agency's projects.

Bibliography

Government sources and references

Czech Development Agency (2015), Powerpoint presentation on "Czech Republic's Support to International Development" given at the Summer School on Globalisation 3.0, Prague.

GoCR (2010), *The Act on Development Cooperation and Humanitarian Aid, and Amending Related Laws*, Government of the Czech Republic, Prague.

MFA (2016a), *Czech Development Cooperation Plan in 2016 and Estimates for 2017 and 2018,* Ministry of Foreign Affairs, Prague, available online at: www.mzv.cz/jnp/en/foreign_relations/development_cooperation_and_humanitarian/information_statistics_publications/czech_development_cooperation_plan_for.html.

MFA (2016b), Draft Concept Note: Implementation of bilateral international development co-operation after 2017, unpublished, unofficial translation from the Czech language into English (Google translate).

MFA (2016c), "OECD Development Assistance Committee peer review: memorandum of the Czech Republic", unpublished, Ministry of Foreign Affairs, Prague.

MFA (2014), *Report from the Complex Evaluation of the Development Cooperation of the Czech Republic in the Sector of Water Supply and Sanitation in Ethiopia*, Ministry of Foreign Affairs, Prague.

MFA (ongoing), evaluations of projects available at: www.mzv.cz/jnp/en/search/index$219343.html?text=evaluation.

Supreme Audit Office (2015), *Central Budget Resources Allocated to External Development Cooperation*, Prague, unpublished.

Chapter 5: The Czech Republic's development co-operation delivery and partnerships

Budgeting and programming processes

Indicator: These processes support quality aid as defined in Busan

The Czech Republic is committed to the principles of effective development as agreed in the Busan Partnership for Effective Development Co-operation. Its emphasis on country ownership is evident in its programme and project methodology. Budgeting gives partners an element of multi-year predictability. The Ministry of Foreign Affairs and the Agency have gained experience with the current set of modalities for delivering Czech ODA and are well aware of their limits. As the Ministry prepares the next generation of country strategy papers it should review its mix of instruments and explore new ways to deliver programmes and projects that build and use partner systems, raise sustainability and impact, and are untied.

There is a limited flexibility to reallocate resources between budget lines

The Czech Republic has made some progress towards multi-year predictability. The annual development co-operation plan, which includes a rolling two-year outlook, is shared with partners (MFA 2016a). Once the Czech Republic has a clear medium-term growth plan for its ODA (Chapter 3) it can boost predictability by integrating the projected budget increase for partner countries or territories into the annual planning cycle. It can also facilitate partners' budget planning by sharing the financial plans with them, including those countries from which Czech ODA will be phased out (Chapters 2 and 3).

There are a number of constraints in the current projectised approach to budgeting and financial planning which reduce flexibility, can undermine sustainability, increase administrative costs, and create uncertainty for implementing partners. For example, the annual development co-operation plan is very detailed, with specific budget lines by country and sector; aid can only be partly reallocated between budget lines in some country programmes.

While three-year projects are increasingly common, the Agency still has to prepare a new contract for each year of the project. It only releases new funds when the new contract is agreed, which can cause delays. Partners in Moldova and Ethiopia mentioned that this aspect of project financing is a challenge because they have to deliver the annual contract and the associated budget in a relatively short time-frame (Annex C). Moreover, financing and auditing rules require detailed reporting and proof of expenditure for all projects and tenders. The rules do not differentiate between the project size or the professional capabilities of the implementer (e.g. to conduct their own audits). Given the number of small projects, this imposes heavy administrative costs on implementing partners and the Czech Development Agency. Finally, budgets for tenders must be spent within the year and companies are required to pay a contractual fine if the project activities are not executed according to the contract.

The Czech Republic identifies projects through close consultation with partner government and local authorities

The Czech Republic has been learning from its first round of multi-year country programmes with priority countries or territories. These programmes are a useful tool for discussing and agreeing on priorities with partner governments and the associated memorandum of understanding. Country ownership is built through consultations with partner government line ministries and local authorities, helping to ensure programmes meet local priorities (Annex C).

However, the links between the Czech Republic's country programmes and its projects are not always clear. The priorities in country programmes are broad and only apply to projects delivered by the Czech Development Agency (CzDA). This makes it difficult to guide project selection and to focus all Czech ODA going to the country (Chapter 4). There is scope to make better use of country programmes to match Czech co-operation to partner countries' or territories' development priorities, to increase focus and coherence between projects, and to develop more programme-based approaches. This is confirmed by feedback from Ethiopia and Moldova, where partners commented that Czech co-operation would have more impact if it were more focused and involved bigger projects.

The MFA and CzDA are continuously improving programming and project procedures with input from Czech non-governmental organisations (NGOs) and embassy staff. The project cycle manual is comprehensive and sets out roles and responsibilities as well as templates for proposals and reporting (MFA, 2011). According to the audit of the Supreme Audit Office, project design is improving in terms of its focus on having a sustainable impact.

The Czech Republic does not yet use country systems

With the exception of its aid to the West Bank and Gaza Strip and local procurement in some priority countries or territories for small-scale tenders, the Czech Republic does not use partner systems for programme design, management, expenditure, monitoring or reporting. According to the 2010 Act on Development Co-operation and Humanitarian Aid, the Agency is not authorised to channel grants through non-Czech entities (GoCR, 2010). It tries, therefore, to provide Czech solutions directly. If this is not possible, it will deliver aid through multilateral organisations (multi-bi) and might join a multi-donor programme. In exceptional situations, such as Afghanistan, the Czech Republic provided sector budget support through a trust fund.

The Czech Republic could look into finding ways to use and strengthen country systems and still get visibility for its support. The small volume of resources should not be an obstacle to using partner systems, putting aid on budget and engaging in programme-based approaches. The Czech Republic could, for example, ear-mark its support to a project within a sector programme, fill gaps in expertise through technical assistance or pilot new ideas that could be scaled up, or support institutional reform in a priority sector (Annex C). Giving local partners responsibility for managing Czech-supported projects – with appropriate oversight by the Agency – could also save on administrative costs and increase ownership but the legal framework may need to be amended to do this (Chapter 4).

Once the Agency decentralises operations to partner countries or territories, it should be better placed to identify and partner with local organisations (Chapter 4). However, it will need a clear mandate and guidelines for deciding when and how to use country systems and public sector instruments.

Risks and opportunities are not assessed systematically from a development perspective

The Czech Republic does not yet have a systematic approach to analysing or managing risks to achieving its overall strategic priorities. It appears to take a narrow view of risks (limited to fiduciary and security risks). However, the current approach to delivering aid through stand-alone projects also poses risks such as undermining partner ownership and reducing sustainability once the project ends. These risks were also identified in the Audit report and evaluations.

The Ministry of Foreign Affairs and the CzDA are planning to conduct more thorough risk assessments at the start of projects, with a focus on sustainability. As it develops this approach, the Czech Republic should also consider systematically analysing the risks and opportunities in delivering the overall strategic objectives of Czech development co-operation and how they will affect development results.

High levels of tied aid stem from a legal requirement

The Czech Republic should step up efforts to untie its aid, in line with Busan commitments to "accelerate efforts to untie aid" (OECD, 2011a). In 2014, the share of untied ODA (excluding administrative costs and in-donor refugee costs) decreased to 32.4% from 40.1% in 2013 – far below the 2014 Development Assistance Committee (DAC) average of 80.6%.

While some public tenders take place in partner countries or territories and attract local companies, there is a financial ceiling of CZK 2 million (about EUR 74 000). The grant scheme, which accounts for 40% of bilateral aid, is fully tied, due to the legal requirement that aid can only be channelled through entities registered in the Czech Republic.

The Ministry of Foreign Affairs is planning to identify the legal amendments required to untie aid further. A key challenge for the MFA and the CzDA will be to convince the government and key stakeholders that untying aid increases value for money and local ownership, which in turn can boost efficiency and impact on the ground. Evidence cited by the OECD shows that tied aid "can increase the costs of a development project by as much as 15 to 30 percent" (Clay, E. J. et al, 2010).

No conditions are attached to projects

The Czech Republic's does not attach policy or any other conditions on its development co-operation.

Partnerships

Indicator: The member makes appropriate use of co-ordination arrangements, promotes strategic partnerships to develop synergies, and enhances mutual accountability

The Czech Republic is a valued development partner. Despite its limited resources and capacity in the field it works well with the government and development partners in key sectors. The next step, as it understands the limits of its current modalities in terms of development impact, will be for the Czech Republic to work through strategic partnerships. To do this, it will need to develop the right policies, tools and instruments.

Division of labour and joint approaches are pragmatic and reflect capacity

In partner countries or territories, the "development diplomats" participate in policy dialogue and co-ordination arrangements and engage in EU joint programming processes. For example, the Czech Republic is leading the joint analysis of the social sectors in Moldova (Annex C). The Czech Republic also tries to avoid duplication with other development co-operation providers. In some instances, the embassy and the Agency try to work closely with other development providers where respective projects have similar objectives but through a project approach. In Moldova, for example, the Czech Republic fits its project within broader efforts by collaborating with Austria and Switzerland (Annex C). However, Czech rules and procedures hinder its contribution to pooled funds and provision of programme funding (Chapter 4). A stronger field presence and delegated authority would maximise its contributions and visibility in more harmonised arrangements. Participating in donor groups would also allow for exchanges with other providers about the context and how they manage projects and different modalities.

Accountability is a work in progress

In addition to the various global accountability reports to which it contributes (MFA, 2016b), the Czech Republic places strong emphasis on responding to partners' priorities and being accountable for delivering on its commitments. The partner government – including central and line ministries and local authorities – is the first port of call for the embassy when identifying new projects. However, given the small scale of projects, the transaction costs of involving line ministries in project committees and monitoring processes can be high. Moreover, as pointed out in the audit of the Czech Supreme Audit office, the Memorandum of Understanding which are signed with the partner government do not have a legal status and this can limit ownership and accountability. Mutual accountability could also be improved by sharing monitoring reports systematically with local partners.

Strategic partnerships will require new tools and instruments

The Czech Republic's current approach to development co-operation needs to be adapted if it is to engage in strategic partnerships with a broader range of government and non-government partners. Its current dependency on Czech NGOs and businesses to deliver most bilateral aid limits the range of projects it can implement, notably when Czech entities do not have the capacity, expertise, or absorption capacity to respond to partners' demands or align with their systems. As the bilateral aid budget increases, the MFA and CzDA should also find ways to work with different partners through other modalities. By having a mix of instruments for delivering the programme it can be more flexible in the way it responds to the priorities of its partner countries or territories.

Transitioning from contract-based co-operation to working through strategic partnerships over the long term will also require new tools and instruments that are results focused (Chapter 6). As it develops its partnership approach, the MFA and the CzDA can learn from other DAC members. For example, the DAC Peer Learning Exercise on Working with the Private Sector in Development Co-operation could be a useful source of good practices.

There is scope to develop new, more strategic ways of engaging with and supporting civil society

The Czech Republic values civil society as one of the foundations of a functioning democratic system (MFA, n.d.). Czech civil society is a key asset and an integral part of development co-operation. It implements about 45% of bilateral aid projects and the government benefits from civil society's development knowledge, experience and policy analysis.

Czech NGOs are also crucial advocates for development co-operation with politicians and the public. They play a watchdog role and challenge the government to deliver on its aid targets and commitments to development effectiveness.

The government has strengthened this sector through its support for capacity building. So-called trilateral co-operation – whereby the CzDA co-finances up to 25% of a NGO project which has another funder e.g. the EU – is an effective way to invest in larger projects. It is also a form of programme support to NGOs and adds weight to their applications to the EU. In 2014, 37 NGO projects were supported by the EU with co-funding from the Czech Agency. The capacity of several Czech NGOs has grown over the years and many of them have a good track record. The local civil society partners of Czech NGOs have also demonstrated their capacity to deliver.

The Ministry of Foreign Affairs is well-placed to build on these positive trends by developing a strategic framework for partnering with civil society and using more effective funding mechanisms, as outlined in the DAC's "12 Lessons for Partnering with Civil Society" (OECD, 2011b). A good starting point could be to prepare an overarching civil society policy that applies to all Czech development co-operation. The policy could build on the Transition Policy, which prioritises strengthening civil society in developing countries, in line with the Busan Partnership (MFA, n.d.). The Czech Republic should also consider developing more predictable, flexible and results-oriented ways of partnering with Czech and non-Czech civil society in its development co-operation.

Fragile states

Indicator: Delivery modalities and partnerships help deliver quality

The Czech Republic does not have a specific strategy or approach to addressing conflict and fragility. However, it does have projects in states that are fragile. While its criteria for selecting partner countries or territories reflect an awareness of the inherent risks, its policies and programmes could reflect issues of fragility better, including by taking a more holistic approach to development and humanitarian assistance in these countries.

Criteria for selecting partner countries or territories take fragility into account

Addressing fragility is not a policy priority of Czech development co-operation. Nevertheless, in 2014, six of its top 10 ODA recipients were conflict-affected or fragile states, compared to four in 2011.[1] The Czech Republic's experience in Afghanistan seems to have influenced its approach to conflict-affected states (Box 5.1). Despite this experience, it has not developed new comprehensive peacebuilding country strategies. In Mali for instance, its military and civilian engagement are not joined together in a comprehensive strategy.

The Czech Republic's criteria for selecting partner countries or territories include the readiness of a country to accept assistance and its ability to engage in political dialogue. These criteria are relevant for fragile states, where the government may require a substantial amount of technical expertise to ensure a constructive partnership.

Nevertheless, while the Czech Republic is aware of fragility in its partner countries or territories, it tends to focus on "less fragile" regions within countries, for example in Ethiopia (Annex C). The Czech Republic's development co-operation strategy and programme in partner countries or territories could be strengthened through more systematic analysis of the drivers of fragility, including climate change. Understanding these drivers is crucial for national policy dialogue, as well as for understanding risks to the Czech Republic programme.

The Czech Republic co-ordinates with other donors and supports multi-donor trust funds

The Czech Republic engages actively with other bilateral development partners to either maximise or sustain its support in fragile or crisis situations – mainly in the form of humanitarian assistance. For instance, it is discussing with the Slovak Republic how to support its education programme in South Sudan as the Slovak Republic withdraws. The Czech Republic is also a contributor to international trust funds, for example, the EU Africa Trust Fund (USD 0.83 million) and the EU Regional Trust Fund in Response to the Syrian Crisis (USD 5.59 million).

Box 5.1: Delivering development during conflict: Experiences in Afghanistan's Logar province

In 2008, as part of the International Security Assistance Force coalition, the Czech Republic took responsibility for the Provincial Reconstruction Team (PRT) of Logar province. The Czech civilian team had 12 construction engineers, agricultural, security and media experts, and was one of the PRTs with the largest civilian presence. Over the next five years the PRT implemented 138 reconstruction and development projects and 107 quick impact projects. Yet attacks on PRT projects were regular and most development projects have now ceased. In 2016, the province has been ranked as the eighth most insecure in Afghanistan – humanitarian needs are assessed as severe. Current Czech interventions in Afghanistan are no longer located in Logar province, mainly for security reasons.

Source: OCHA (2015), 2016 Humanitarian Response Plan, *https://docs.unocha.org/sites/dms/Afghanistan/afg_2016_hrp_final_20160107.pdf; MFA (2013), "The Afghan mission of Czech PRT in Logar is over after five years", http://afghanistan.mzv.cz/prtlogar/en/news/the_afghan_mission_of_czech_prt_in_logar.html, Ministry of Defence (2013), "ISAF PRT", www.army.cz/scripts/detail.php?id=87800.*

Use of multilateral channels eases the burden on partner governments

The Czech Republic has no specific delivery mechanisms for fragile states. However, it pays attention to the aid effectiveness principles. Development and humanitarian funds are mainly delivered through multilateral channels, allowing its aid to fit into international state-building strategies, in particular within the EC policy framework. In countries where human and management resources are often under strain, this avoids multiple country strategies and helps the partner country or territory government to better manage the flow of development co-operation resources.

Notes

1. In 2011, fragile states or territories such as Afghanistan, Bosnia & Herzegovina, Ethiopia, the West Bank and Gaza Strip were amongst the Czech Republic's top 10 ODA recipients (a total of USD 19.63 million). In 2014, Afghanistan, Bosnia & Herzegovina, Ethiopia, Kosovo, Syria and Ukraine were amongst its top 10 recipients of ODA (a total of USD 25.5 million) (MFA, 2014).

Bibliography

Government sources

GoCR (2010), *Act on Development Cooperation and Humanitarian Aid, and Amending Related Laws*, Government of the Czech Republic, Prague.

MFA (2016a), *Czech Development Cooperation Plan in 2016 and Estimates for 2017 and 2018,* Ministry of Foreign Affairs, Prague, available online at: www.mzv.cz/jnp/en/foreign_relations/development_cooperation_and_humanitarian/information_statistics_publications/czech_development_cooperation_plan_for.html.

MFA (2016b), "OECD Development Assistance Committee peer review: memorandum of the Czech Republic", (unpublished), Ministry of Foreign Affairs, Prague.

MFA (2010-2015), Czech Development Cooperation Plans 2010-2015, Ministry of Foreign Affairs, Prague, www.mzv.cz/jnp/en/foreign_relations/development_cooperation_and_humanitarian/information_statistics_publications/czech_development_cooperation_plan_for.html.

MFA (2013), "The Afghan mission of Czech PRT in Logar is over after five years", Ministry of Foreign Affairs, Prague, http://afghanistan.mzv.cz/prtlogar/en/news/the_afghan_mission_of_czech_prt_in_logar.html.

MFA (2011), Methodology of Project Cycle Management for Bilateral Development Cooperation of the Czech Republic, Ministry of Foreign Affairs, Prague, www.mzv.cz/jnp/cz/zahranicni_vztahy/rozvojova_spoluprace/koncepce_publikace/koncepce/metodika_projektoveho_cyklu.html.

MFA (2010), *The Development Cooperation Strategy of the Czech Republic 2010-2017*, Ministry of Foreign Affairs, Prague.

MFA (n.d.), *Transition Policy,* Ministry of Foreign Affairs, Prague.

Ministry of Defence (2013), "ISAF PRT", Ministry of Defence & Armed Forces, Prague www.army.cz/scripts/detail.php?id=87800.

OCHA (2015), *2016 Humanitarian Response Plan,* United Nations Office for Coordination of Humanitarian Affairs, Geneva, https://docs.unocha.org/sites/dms/Afghanistan/afg_2016_hrp_final_20160107.pdf.

Other sources

Clay, Edward J., Matthew Geddes and Luisa Natali: *Untying Aid: Is it working? An Evaluation of the Implementation of the Paris Declaration and of the 2001 DAC Recommendation of Untying ODA to the LDCs*, Copenhagen, December 2009.

OECD (2011a),"Busan Partnership for Effective Development Co-operation", Fourth High Level Forum on Aid Effectiveness, Busan, Republic of Korea, 29 November-1 December 2011, www.oecd.org/dac/effectiveness/49650173.pdf.

OECD (2011b) Partnering with Civil Society: 12 Lessons from DAC Peer Reviews, www.oecd.org/dac/peer-reviews/12%20Lessons%20Partnering%20with%20Civil%20Society.pdf.

Chapter 6: Results management and accountability of Czech development co-operation

Results-based management system

Indicator: A results-based management system is in place to assess performance on the basis of development priorities, objectives and systems of partner countries or territories

Having in place a more comprehensive results-based management system would help the Czech Republic to ensure that it is getting the most out of investments, to learn from and improve the quality of programmes, and to communicate the results of its development co-operation efforts to Parliament and the public. The forthcoming medium-term development co-operation strategy and the next generation of country strategy programmes, together with the 2030 Agenda, can help set the results framework. Building a results culture and strengthening internal capacity will be critical in making the move towards managing for development results, as agreed in Busan.

The Czech Republic needs a systematic approach to managing for results

The Czech Republic is aware of the importance of managing for development results in order to be sure it is getting the most out of its investments, to take evidence-based decisions and for communication and accountability to taxpayers and partners. Good foundations are in place for building a comprehensive system of managing for results that links results at various levels: project, programme and overall strategy. The sound and evolving project cycle methodology, for example, introduced results in project identification and monitoring. The Czech Republic also uses evaluation findings to improve project and programme management.

While the Agency is making progress with managing for results at the project level, the Ministry of Foreign Affairs, in co-ordination with the Council for Development Cooperation, needs, in particular, to clarify measurable results that the Czech Republic wants to achieve at the strategic level. It has an opportunity to do this with the next medium-term development co-operation strategy and in the new country strategy programmes that will be prepared in the next couples of year. By linking its results frameworks with the Sustainable Development Goals (SDGs), the Czech Republic will also be better placed to show how its development co-operation is contributing to Agenda 2030 at the strategic level and to development results and mutual accountability in partner countries or territories.

Like in other Development Assistance Committee (DAC) countries, institutionalising and building a culture of managing for results for strengthened accountability and informed decision making is a challenge. Awareness-raising, training and other incentives can help advance this agenda. This is a work-in-progress in the Czech Republic: it is starting to build awareness of how to manage for results and technical capacity for measuring results, for example, in setting baselines, and output and outcome indicators. By engaging with the OECD DAC results community, it can share and learn from members' experience and good practice in managing for results.

The Agency is starting to shift from financial and activity control to measuring progress against outputs and outcomes

While the co-operation strategies for programme countries do not include specific goals or results indicators, the Agency has taken important first steps in managing for development results at the project level. All new projects must include a logical framework, and the Agency has prepared two pilot sector programmes that include results to be achieved – drawing from partners' strategies – and measurable indicators. Where available, the Agency uses existing results indicators set out by partner countries or territories, which is good practice.

The Agency monitors its bilateral projects and programmes by analysing implementing partners' reports and through monitoring missions carried out twice a year by embassies or Agency experts. Monitoring practices are still largely about control, although they are gradually paying more attention to results. The introduction of logframes has helped to reconstruct baselines for measuring project outcomes and the new forms for individual project monitoring are more focused on results. Information from monitoring missions and reports is used to adjust programme and project management processes when needed.

There is no specific approach to monitoring results in fragile states

The Czech Republic's development co-operation policy is not focused on fragility even if it delivers aid in countries that are considered to be fragile (Chapter 5). In light of this, it does not have a specific approach to monitoring the conflict sensitivity of its programmes and projects in these contexts. As fragile contexts are volatile, monitoring the effect of the overall programme on the drivers of conflicts or crises, along with measurable deliverables, could enhance results in these contexts.

Evaluation system

Indicator: The evaluation system is in line with the DAC evaluation principles

The Czech Republic has made good progress in institutionalising evaluation in its development co-operation system. It has a dedicated Evaluation Unit, an annual plan and a specific budget. Staffing of the unit is limited, however. Next steps for strengthening evaluation include formulating a policy and ensuring the independence of evaluations from development policy and programming, in line with DAC principles and guidelines.

The Czech Republic is institutionalising evaluation; a dedicated policy would strengthen it

Since 2012, the Division of Humanitarian Assistance and Evaluation within the Department of Development Cooperation and Humanitarian Assistance has been responsible for evaluation. The unit in charge of evaluation has a single staff member responsible for all evaluation procedures together with other duties. This means that the evaluation manager can manage a few (3 – 6) strategic evaluations in a given year.[1]

The project cycle methodology (MFA, 2011) describes the purpose and procedure of evaluating projects and programmes; the role and responsibilities of the Ministry of Foreign Affairs and of the department in charge of evaluation; the role of other actors; the procedures for appointing a reference group for evaluation within the Council for Development Cooperation and for selecting evaluators, evaluation missions and for producing final reports. While this is useful, it is not framed by an explicit evaluation policy in line with DAC evaluation principles. The system would benefit from a policy that sets out the institutional arrangements for ensuring the independence of the evaluation unit and that defines the overall strategic purpose of evaluation, including in relation to the overall strategy and system itself.

The independence of evaluation from policy and programming could be reinforced

The Czech Republic supports the independence of individual evaluations by commissioning independent evaluators[2] and through the special role played by the Council for Development Cooperation and its Evaluation Working Group.[3] In addition, a reference group of experts[4] is appointed for each evaluation to control the quality of evaluation reports and ensure the relevance of findings. These arrangements support credibility in a resource constrained environment, however the reporting line for the evaluation function is such that there is a risk of conflict of interest between policy, programming and evaluation which could undermine its independence.[5] As the Czech Republic continues to institutionalise evaluation, it should review and identify how to guarantee the overall independence of the evaluation function.

There is a dedicated evaluation budget and plan

Evaluations are financed through a dedicated budget that is earmarked in the Annual Plan for Development Cooperation (MFA, 2016). The evaluation plan is prepared annually by the Ministry of Foreign Affairs, in collaboration with the Agency, and submitted to the Evaluation Working Group of the Council for Development Cooperation for discussion. The plan is then approved by the Council for Development Cooperation and published on the Ministry of Foreign Affairs' website. When deciding what to evaluate, the ministry tries to ensure adequate coverage of priority countries, territories and the main sectors, while also responding to specific learning needs.[6] Being clearer about why and when activities are to be evaluated, based on risk or "need-to-know", would help ensure limited resources are spent strategically.

Involving aid beneficiaries in the evaluation process is challenging

The Czech Republic recognises that involving aid recipients in evaluations is a challenge, as for many DAC members. Some efforts have been made to make the evaluation process more inclusive by sharing terms of reference – published in Czech and English since 2015 – and final reports with the embassies. Embassies can respond and share reports with partners and local evaluation networks. Furthermore, according to the Czech authorities local stakeholders are engaged in evaluation design, local experts are part of the evaluation teams and evaluators are required to present the preliminary findings of each evaluation in the partner country or territory. A practical way of stepping up the involvement of stakeholders could be to invite them to become members of evaluation reference groups. This is common practice for other DAC members (OECD, forthcoming).

Institutional learning

Indicator: Evaluations and appropriate knowledge management systems are used as management tools

There is a strong culture of learning in Czech development co-operation. Reviews, monitoring and evaluations are key tools for improving the quality and management of development interventions. The MFA and the Agency could do more to consolidate the knowledge coming from different sources and networks and make it accessible to all staff involved in development at headquarters and in embassies.

The Czech Republic uses evaluation findings to improve its practices

The Czech Republic disseminates evaluation results in a systematic and transparent manner by presenting and discussing evaluation reports in seminars and by publishing them on the Ministry of Foreign Affairs' website.[7] Both the Czech Development Agency (CzDA) and the ministry respond to evaluation recommendations formally in a written management response. Recommendations are subsequently implemented through standard procedures and project management. This was confirmed in the audit by the

Supreme Audit Office (Supreme Audit Office, 2015).[8] Follow up of recommendations is ensured by the Evaluation Working Group under the Council for Development Cooperation, which monitors whether they have been implemented. The Czech Republic is learning from evaluation results and recommendations and adapting its policies and practices. It should continue in this spirit.

Knowledge sharing occurs through informal channels

Knowledge sharing in the Czech system is facilitated by the small size of the community, as well as general good will and interest in learning from experience. Channels for sharing knowledge include:

- informal exchanges between MFA and Agency staff
- workshops organised to present evaluation findings and other reports
- meetings of the Council for Development Cooperation, to which non-governmental organisations (NGOs), the private sector, the Czech Evaluation Society and research institutions bring their own experience and knowledge
- participation in international networks such as the Practitioners Network for Development Co-operation and UNDP knowledge-sharing programme.

Nevertheless, the Czech Republic would benefit from a more centralised system for capturing, saving and disseminating knowledge and information that can be accessed by all relevant actors at headquarters and in the field. While informal knowledge sharing is useful and should be nurtured, it can become more difficult when staff numbers increase, it depends on the good will of individuals and it can be lost when staff move on.

The Agency has recently developed a new information tool which aims to become a library of all project information. It offers potential for spreading good practice. As it develops this tool it should be mindful that finding effective software/electronic solutions for sharing knowledge is still a challenge for many DAC members (OECD, forthcoming).

Communication, accountability and development awareness

Indicator: The member communicates development results transparently and honestly

The Czech Republic is committed to increasing transparency in line with its Busan commitment. To gain public and political support for its co-operation programme, it needs to communicate strategically and coherently about development policy and activities, focusing on achievements and challenges, and drawing on results. The MFA and the Agency can reinforce communication and the overall visibility of Czech co-operation by developing and delivering common messages and reinforcing partnerships with key stakeholders to raise awareness of development issues.

The Czech Republic is strongly committed to transparency

Since joining the DAC, the Czech Republic has improved the transparency of its development co-operation programme.[9] It provides high quality and timely statistical information to the DAC on its ODA. Nevertheless, the Aid Transparency Index "Publish What You Fund" rated Czech transparency as poor in 2014.[10] For technical reasons the Czech Republic is not yet publishing information according to the Busan Common Standard, but it is committed to implementing the standard for the electronic publication of timely, comprehensive and forward-looking information when the technical problems in its reporting system are resolved.

Coherent communication is essential for public and political support

In a 2015 Special Eurobarometer Survey (EU, 2016), 78% of respondents in the Czech Republic said it was very important or fairly important to help people in developing countries – lower than the EU average of 89%. The Czech Republic is conscious of the importance of maintaining and reinforcing public support for development co-operation as a prerequisite for political backing for its co-operation programme.

Plans at the MFA and the Agency to develop more strategic and targeted communication about development co-operation respond to the need for better-informed public opinion and support. Communication capacity within the Agency has been reinforced, and it is preparing a new communication strategy. This is timely – with the MFA also preparing the new development co-operation strategy, there is an opportunity to develop a coherent narrative for Czech development co-operation. Good practice suggests that effective public engagement requires clear, coherent messages that go beyond isolated events, facts or statistics to communicate on long-term progress and effectiveness (OECD, 2013). The strategy could also identify a comprehensive, coherent and targeted approach to raising awareness of the entire Czech development co-operation system, thereby avoiding inconsistent messages and competition for visibility.

The Czech Republic invests in global education

Global development education is an important priority for the Czech Republic.[11] Despite the solidarity that the Czechs show during humanitarian crises, the MFA considers public awareness of extreme poverty and of the importance of long-term development co-operation and a host of other related issues to be insufficient (MFA, 2010b).

The Ministry of Foreign Affairs and Ministry of Education are responsible for the overall National Strategy for Global Development Education 2011-17[12] and the Agency manages a global education grant scheme for NGOs. The Czech Republic builds on the historical role that these organisations play in "offering a wide range of global education and awareness-building activities" within the country (MFA, 2010b).[13] Research institutes also play an important role in building understanding of specific development issues, especially policy coherence for development. The Czech Republic should continue to build on its good practice in global education, notably by partnering with civil society and the Ministry of Education, Youth and Sports. By leveraging partnerships with these organisations it will broaden the reach and impact of global education (OECD, 2013).

Notes

1. The evaluation plan for 2016 can be found at www.mzv.cz/jnp/en/foreign_relations/development_cooperation_and_humanitarian/bilateral_development_cooperation/evaluation/evaluations_of_czech_development_1.html.

2. Evaluations are commissioned through public procurement and the terms of reference are published on the MFA's website.

3. This working group, responsible for supervising the evaluation processes, discusses the annual evaluation plan and the terms of reference, and oversees the follow-up to the recommendations.

4. Reference groups are composed of volunteers from line ministries, NGOs, academics and representatives of the private sector. In addition, an independent expert on evaluation methodology from the Czech Evaluation Society participates in all reference groups (OECD, forthcoming).

5. External evaluators report to the Ministry of Foreign Affairs and the evaluation manager reports to the head of the Division of Humanitarian Assistance and Evaluation, who is in charge of humanitarian policy and is deputy head of the Development Cooperation Department.

6. For instance, the CzDA asked to evaluate specific projects before writing its new sectoral strategy for Moldova.

7. Evaluation reports are mostly published in Czech with executive summaries in English. English summaries can be found at www.mzv.cz/jnp/en/foreign_relations/development_cooperation_and_humanitarian/bilateral_development_cooperation/evaluation/index.html.

8. For instance, evaluation recommendations led the CzDA to prepare two pilot sector programmes, and to replicate a successful project carried out in Cambodia to Zambia. A recommendation from the meta-evaluation of the Czech evaluation system led to the terms of reference for evaluations to be improved to ensure more concrete and applicable recommendations.

9. All ODA information (including statistics; strategies; plans; budget; programmes and projects; and evaluations) is available on the MFA and CzDA websites.

10. More information available at: http://ati.publishwhatyoufund.org/2014/donor/czech-republic/.

11. There is also a dedicated working group that permanently reviews the implementation of the national Global Development Education Strategy.

12. The National Strategy for Global Development Education 2011-2015 has been extended to 2017. It aims to "provide all citizens of the Czech Republic with access to information on developing countries and global development and to inspire them to take an active role in tackling global issues as well as issues faced by the developing world" through inclusion of global development education principles and topics in lifelong learning and educational programmes across all levels of the Czech system of education (MFA, 2010b).

13. Including within the Czech Parliament.

Bibliography

Government sources

MFA (2016), "OECD Development Assistance Committee peer review: memorandum of the Czech Republic", unpublished, Ministry of Foreign Affairs, Prague.

MFA (2010a), *The Development Cooperation Strategy of the Czech Republic 2010-2017,* Ministry of Foreign Affairs, Prague, www.mzv.cz/jnp/en/foreign_relations/development_cooperation_and_humanitarian/development_cooperation_strategy_of_the.html.

MFA (2010b), *National Strategy for Global Development Education 2011-2015,* Ministry of Foreign Affairs, Prague, www.mzv.cz/jnp/en/foreign_relations/development_cooperation_and_humanitarian/general_information/national_strategy_for_global_development.html.

Other sources

EU (2016), "The European Year for Development – Citizens' views on development, cooperation and aid", *Special Eurobarometer* 441, December 2015, http://ec.europa.eu/europeaid/sites/devco/files/sp441-devco-report-final_en.pdf.

OECD (forthcoming), *OECD DAC Review of Evaluation Systems*, OECD Publishing, Paris.

OECD (2014), *Measuring and Managing Results in Development Co-operation: A Review of Challenges and Practices among DAC Members*, OECD, Paris, https://www.oecd.org/dac/peer-reviews/Measuring-and-managing-results.pdf.

OECD (2013), *Engaging with the Public: 12 Lessons from DAC Peer Reviews and the Network of DAC Development Communicators*, OECD, Paris, https://www.oecd.org/dac/peer-reviews/12%20Lessons%20Engaging%20with%20the%20public.pdf.

OECD (2010), *Evaluation in Development Agencies, Better Aid,* OECD Publishing, Paris, DOI: http://dx.doi.org/10.1787/9789264094857-en.

Supreme Audit Office (2015), Central Budget Resources Allocated to External Development Cooperation, Prague, unpublished.

Chapter 7: The Czech Republic's humanitarian assistance

Strategic framework

Indicator: Clear political directives and strategies for resilience, response and recovery

The Czech Republic's overall policy framework for humanitarian aid, which is relatively new, is solid and driven by international standards. However, the strategic framework could better reflect the complexity of protracted crises where humanitarian assistance, development co-operation and security concerns intertwine.

There is a solid policy framework for humanitarian programming

The overall policy framework derives from the Act on Development Cooperation and Humanitarian Aid (GoCR, 2010), as well as the Development Cooperation Strategy of the Czech Republic 2010-2017 (MFA, 2010), both adopted in 2010. The humanitarian strategy is driven by international humanitarian laws, the Good Humanitarian Donorship principles (GHD, 2003) and the EU consensus on humanitarian aid (EU, 2007). Although based on fairly broad objectives, it provides a principled – neutral and impartial – approach to humanitarian interventions. The Development Cooperation Strategy refers to the interconnections between humanitarian aid and development co-operation as does the annual humanitarian assistance plan which is prepared by Ministry of Foreign Affairs (MFA, 2015a).

Strategies could reflect better the Czech Republic's coherent engagement in complex emergencies

The 2010-2017 Development Cooperation Strategy refers to humanitarian aid as a two year initial step after a crisis.[1] However, many crises are protracted over several years. This is something the Czech Republic is experiencing in Ukraine and the Middle East. In these cases humanitarian needs and development priorities interlink. The Czech Republic could update its strategy paper to reflect its own practice of bringing together emergency and longer-term response in complex emergencies.

Disaster risk reduction is rooted in development co-operation

Humanitarian funds for disaster risk reduction activities are quite limited in the Czech Republic. They usually become available in the last quarter of the year if no other priority has emerged and as part of the Czech Republic's response to disasters. In its priority countries or territories, the Czech Republic integrates disaster risk reduction in the development co-operation programme – often as follow-up to humanitarian disaster response in these countries. This approach to disaster risk reduction as part of development co-operation can help ensure a more sustainable impact while also preserving the relatively small humanitarian budget for other priorities. In Ethiopia, for example, the Czech Republic's environmental geology programme takes a long-term perspective which allows it to build solid and sustainable expertise in this area.

A stable but limited budget

The humanitarian budget is limited, but stable, with annual allocations of CZK 73 million (USD 3 million) since 2010 (MFA, 2015b). Since 2014, the humanitarian budget has also received additional allocations from the government to respond to specific crises. For instance, extra funds for Ukraine and the Ebola outbreak in 2015 added 23% to the initial budget.

The ongoing refugee and migration crisis is having a direct effect on the Czech Republic's humanitarian budget. CZK 10 million (USD 0.4 million) has been drawn from the 2016 humanitarian budget for operations in Greece and Turkey, with no certainty over a supplementary allocation for humanitarian aid operations. The Ministry of Interior (MoI) is also supporting the migration crisis response, reflecting the complexity of this situation, which is at the crossroads between humanitarian aid and migration control. While the Czech Republic reports on its ODA expenditure in this area the dual source of funding (from the MFA and the MoI) in response to this crisis can blur the lines between humanitarian assistance and migration control. It requires careful management so that humanitarian principles continue to guide the humanitarian action.

Effective programme design

Indicator: Programmes target the highest risk to life and livelihood

Whilst the Czech humanitarian strategy and engagement criteria are becoming more solid and coherent, its fragmented approach undermines the impact of its crisis response. The Czech Republic could increase its impact by responding to only a few specific crises, or by creating a comparative advantage by building expertise in a specific humanitarian response sector.

Funding criteria are sound; impact would be greater with more focused and predictable allocations

The Czech Republic responds to large multilateral appeals, for instance from the International Committee of the Red Cross (ICRC) and the UN, and has also been a regular contributor to the Central Emergency Response Fund (CERF) since its inception in 2006.

Since the beginning of the Development Cooperation Strategy in 2010, the Czech Republic funds, on average, 34 projects per year. The humanitarian portfolio remains very broad: funds are dispersed to many crises and countries.[2] This approach enables the Czech Republic to get a good coverage but, given the small budget, it can also limit the impact of its humanitarian response. The Development Cooperation Strategy 2010-2017 emphasised the need for coherence between humanitarian aid and development co-operation in priority countries or territories, however, since 2010 a low average of 11.1% of humanitarian funding was allocated to humanitarian responses in the Czech Republic's priority countries or territories. Having such as broad portfolio also places a substantial administrative burden on the staff member who manages this budget line.

While the humanitarian budget is fragmented, the Ministry of Foreign Affairs selects its humanitarian partners and the programmes it funds strategically. For instance, it supports projects in multilateral organisations which are underfunded or which interest fewer donors.[3] This type of niche approach allows the Czech Republic to maximise its limited humanitarian resources while keeping control over programme design. It is also valued by multilateral partners, who face continual underfunding for certain "forgotten crises" or activities. The Czech Republic could gain greater visibility and focus within the humanitarian environment by concentrating a larger share of its budget on such underfunded crises or sectors.

The annual humanitarian plan divides the spending forecast into quarterly strategic priorities and related disbursements in line with financial rules. However, this has no operational justification. It means that some partners have to wait until the third quarter to receive (limited) Czech funds. Greater focus on fewer crises, while balancing its niche approach with a commitment to multilateral support, would allow Czech humanitarian funds to be allocated in fewer batches and earlier in the year, giving more predictability to partners.

Proper use of the EU early warning system

The Czech Republic uses the EU early warning mechanism and works closely with its representatives in Rome, Geneva, Brussels and New York to ensure early updates on how crises are evolving. This allows for a rapid and co-ordinated response, especially to natural disasters, as witnessed by the 2014 Balkans floods or by the 2015 Nepal earthquake.

Innovative delivery mechanisms can foster greater beneficiary participation

The Czech Republic believes that its small-scale funding favours beneficiary participation in small projects. However, beneficiary participation is not necessarily automatic when supporting international NGOs or multilateral partners. To foster such participation further, and in line with the Grand Bargain[4] provisions, the Czech Republic could consider broadening the number of partners with whom it uses innovative delivery mechanisms, such as cash-based programmes or mobile banking. These mechanisms give beneficiaries greater control over the assistance they receive and imply that relief partners have a greater understanding of how household economies work. Several Czech NGOs were not aware that the Czech Republic supported these mechanisms.

Effective delivery, partnerships and instruments

Indicator: Delivery modalities and partnerships help deliver quality

The Czech Republic has the necessary tools to deliver an adequate humanitarian response. Its rapid response is efficient within the European civil protection mechanism. However, with 34 projects per year on average, its humanitarian assistance to protracted crises is spread too thinly over too many projects. This reduces its visibility and the potential impact of its humanitarian assistance.

Limited funding restricts the ability to link development and humanitarian action

The Czech Republic is striving for closer interaction between humanitarian action and development assistance in its priority countries or territories. Country strategy papers for Afghanistan and Ethiopia emphasise the need to "consolidate the synergy generated by the positive effects of humanitarian intervention and development cooperation" (MFA, 2013). However, the limited humanitarian budget available for recovery activities in priority countries or territories restricts the scope for resilience building and linking development and humanitarian action.

Rapid response tools and mechanisms are in place

The Czech Republic has an efficient crisis co-ordination mechanism involving the Ministry of Interior and the Ministry of Foreign Affairs. This enables an efficient response in particular to natural disasters. Since 2010, it has prepositioned emergency stock in the National Humanitarian Base of Zbiroh's Fire Rescue Service. Solid links with the European civil protection mechanism give the Czech Republic the capacity to deploy this material as well as its experts at short notice (e.g. the Nepal earthquakes, Balkan floods, Ebola virus).

Effective partnerships could be consolidated by financial streamlining

Projects by NGOs registered in the Czech Republic are selected through an annual call for proposals managed centrally in Prague. The government consults the humanitarian NGOs regularly on items of mutual interest. Partners have a chance to make suggestions on the humanitarian strategy at an annual formal meeting – NGOs confirm that the Ministry of Foreign Affairs takes some suggestions on board.

Since the budget is relatively small, NGO partners are as interested in the legitimacy and political support they get from the Czech government's involvement as they are in receiving funding. For instance, government support helps Czech NGOs to get access to larger EC funds through the trilateral co-funding mechanism (Chapter 5). This partnership approach with NGOs could be reinforced further by exploring innovative delivery modalities, concentrating on specific niches, and streamlining the quarterly-based funding mechanism. For instance, a lower number of financial decisions would help partners to manage better their financial planning.

Co-ordination within the EU framework is solid

The Czech Republic takes co-ordination seriously. It is part of the European Committee for Humanitarian and Food Assistance (COHAFA). Memoranda of understanding (MoU) on development co-operation have been signed with other donors, including Austria and the United States (CzDA, 2013). It could also consider having MoU in the humanitarian field, for instance on joint monitoring and analysis.

Organisation fit for purpose

Indicator: Systems, structures, processes and people work together effectively and efficiently

The Czech Republic has a centralised structure and a network of permanent representatives to international organisations informs headquarters about humanitarian issues. However, it is difficult for headquarters to benefit fully from the information and knowledge it receives from this network due to the constraints on staffing. Reinforcing the humanitarian team at headquarters would help the Ministry of Foreign Affairs to respond to the growing need to co-ordinate across government and with an array of other partners for increasingly complex humanitarian crises. There are close working relationships across government on major new humanitarian emergencies, mostly sudden-onset disasters, but more clarity is needed on the role and responsibility of the Ministry of Interior, notably in relation to the Czech Republic's humanitarian response to the migration crisis.

A "whole-of-government" approach to complex crises is still evolving

Co-ordination with the Ministry of Interior is well established. Procedures are clear and efficient, especially for deploying civil protection assets to natural disasters. Up to now, the MFA and the MoI co-operated in an ad hoc way to respond to humanitarian and migration crises. Ways of working should now become more explicit, to give partners and the public a clear overview of the Czech Republic's humanitarian assistance, especially in the Middle East and the Balkans. Co-ordination with other ministries remains ad-hoc, for instance with the Ministry of Health in relation to the Ebola crisis response.

Civil-military co-ordination is based on international standards

While the Czech Republic does not have a specific cross-government civil-military policy regulating the use of military assets to support humanitarian response, the humanitarian strategy is based on the Good Humanitarian Donorship principles (GHD, 2003) and the European consensus on humanitarian aid (EU, 2007). Moreover, before deployment, military personnel are trained by the MFA's International Law Department at the Peacekeeping Forces' training base in Český Krumlov.[5] The Ministry of Defence is also part of the National Committee on International Humanitarian Law.

Insufficient humanitarian staff in headquarters

Czech humanitarian assistance is managed by one person within the MFA who also has other duties within the Department for Development Co-operation and Humanitarian Assistance (Chapter 4). The current staffing limits the capacity to follow an increasingly complex humanitarian environment and to monitor bilateral projects. A reinforced humanitarian team in Prague could also better process information received through the network of representatives to key international organisations and use it to strengthen partnerships.

Results, learning and accountability

Indicator: Results are measured and communicated, and lessons learnt

The Ministry of Foreign Affairs' evaluation plan does not include the humanitarian strategy or programmes. Evaluation of long-term humanitarian responses to protracted and complex crises could yield valuable lessons for the humanitarian strategy. While information on humanitarian activities is available, there is scope to reach out more proactively to the general public in order to improve visibility and enhance public support.

Objectives and performance are not evaluated against the overall strategy

The Czech Republic's overall humanitarian response is controlled and audited through internal control processes, but with the exception of one in 2013, its objectives and performance are not evaluated. The humanitarian strategy is designed annually, incorporating inputs from embassies and partners. However, there are no specific indicators for monitoring the relevance and impact of humanitarian action. Although the budget is limited, the Czech Republic's humanitarian objectives and performance could benefit from being reviewed in light of efforts to have closer links with development co-operation and engagement in the migration crisis.

External evaluation could be used more systematically

The Ministry of Foreign Affairs has an annual external evaluation plan (Chapter 6). However, humanitarian actions are rarely evaluated.[6] The two humanitarian responses that were evaluated so far provided useful information on the relevance, impact and sustainability of the assessed programmes, along with substantial recommendations.[7] Given the limited humanitarian monitoring capacity within embassies and headquarters, external evaluations could be used more systematically for the largest and most complex humanitarian responses.

Humanitarian activities are communicated

Information about the humanitarian strategy, results and funding are available on the MFA's website. This information is also used for staff training. There are also press releases for each new project receiving support. The MFA also participates in public gatherings on humanitarian affairs. There is scope, however, to provide the public with easier access to its more comprehensive information about the humanitarian portfolio.

Notes

1. The immediate response and restoration of basic conditions within two years of a crisis defines humanitarian action in the Czech Republic's Development Co-operation Strategy of 2010-2017. The need for assistance in protracted or complex humanitarian crisis is also mentioned.

2. Since 2010, 204 humanitarian projects were funded by the Czech Republic, with an average of CZK 2.09 million (USD 85 184) (MFA, 2016).

3. Including an education programme for Afghan refugees in Iran with UNHCR (2013), and World Food Program logistics in the Central African Republic (2014).

4. The Czech Republic has signed up to the Grand Bargain – A shared commitment to better serve people in need : www.oecd.org/dac/governance-peace/conflictfragilityandresilience/docs/Grand_Bargain_final_22_May_FINAL-2.pdf.

5. The Czech Republic maintains a military base to prepare units for peace operations abroad. The curriculum encompasses training in international law. More on the training base at: www.ckrumlov.cz/uk/mesto/soucas/t_sfor.htm.

6. In 2016, for instance, seven development projects will be evaluated in four countries in the agriculture, education and civil society support sectors, but no humanitarian response evaluation is foreseen in the external evaluation plan for 2016. See: www.mzv.cz/jnp/en/foreign_relations/development_cooperation_and_humanitarian/bilateral_development_cooperation/evaluation/evaluations_of_czech_development_1.html.

7. In 2013, there was an evaluation of the Czech comprehensive humanitarian support in the aftermath of Cyclone Nargis in Myanmar 2008 – 2011; a development project on maternal and infant health in Cambodia was also evaluated.

Bibliography

Government sources

CzDA (2013), Cooperation with Other Donors, Czech Development Agency, Prague. www.czda.cz/czda/cooperation-with-other-donors.htm?lang=en.

GoCR (2010), Act on Development Cooperation and Humanitarian Aid, and Amending Related Laws, Government of the Czech Republic, Prague.

MFA (2016), "Humanitarian Assistance provided by the Czech Republic in 1995 – 2015", internal document, unpublished, Ministry of Foreign Affairs, Prague.

MFA (2015a), Czech Development Cooperation Plans 2010-2015, Ministry of Foreign Affairs, Prague, www.mzv.cz/jnp/en/foreign_relations/development_cooperation_and_humanitarian/information_statistics_publications/czech_development_cooperation_plan_for.html.

MFA (2015b), Humanitarian Assistance annual reports, webpage, Ministry of Foreign Affairs, Prague, www.mzv.cz/jnp/en/foreign_relations/development_cooperation_and_humanitarian/humanitarian_aid/annual_reports/index.html and correspondence with Ministry of Foreign Affairs.

MFA (2013), Development cooperation programme in Afghanistan and Development cooperation programme in Ethiopia, Ministry of Foreign Affairs, Prague, www.mzv.cz/jnp/en/foreign_relations/development_cooperation_and_humanitarian/bilateral_development_cooperation/programme_countries/index.html.

MFA (2010), The Development Co-operation Strategy of the Czech Republic 2010-2017, Ministry of Foreign Affairs, Prague, www.mzv.cz/jnp/en/foreign_relations/development_cooperation_and_humanitarian/development_cooperation_strategy_of_the.html.

Other sources

GHD (2003), *23 Principles and Good Practice of Humanitarian Donorship,* Declaration made in Stockholm 16-17 June, Good Humanitarian Donorship initiative, www.ghdinitiative.org/ghd/gns/principles-good-practice-of-ghd/principles-good-practice-ghd.html.

EU (2007), European Consensus on Humanitarian Aid, European Union, Brussels, http://ec.europa.eu/echo/files/media/publications/consensus_en.pdf.

Annex A: OECD/DAC standard suite of tables

Table A.1 Total financial flows

USD million at current prices and exchange rates

Czech Republic	2000-04	2005-09	2010	2011	2012	2013	2014
							Net disbursements
Total official flows	57	188	228	250	220	211	217
Official development assistance	57	188	228	250	220	211	212
Bilateral	39	88	79	77	66	57	63
Multilateral	18	100	148	174	153	154	150
Other official flows	-	-	-	-	-	-	5
Bilateral	-	-	-	-	-	-	5
Multilateral	-	-	-	-	-	-	-
Net Private Grants	-	-	-	-	-	-	-
Private flows at market terms	-	-	-	-	-	-	-111
Bilateral: *of which*	-	-	-	-	-	-	-111
Direct investment	-	-	-	-	-	-	-173
Export credits	-	-	-	-	-	-	62
Multilateral	-	-	-	-	-	-	-
Total flows	57	188	228	250	220	211	106
for reference:							
ODA (at constant 2013 USD million)	*100*	*205*	*228*	*233*	*223*	*211*	*219*
ODA (as a % of GNI)	*0.08*	*0.12*	*0.13*	*0.13*	*0.12*	*0.11*	*0.11*
Total flows (as a % of GNI) (a)	*0.08*	*0.12*	*0.13*	*0.12*	*0.12*	*0.11*	*0.06*
ODA to and channelled through NGOs							
- In USD million	-	1	1	17	15	16	15
- In percentage of total net ODA	-	0	0	7	7	8	7
- DAC countries' average % of total net ODA	*9*	*7*	*9*	*13*	*13*	*13*	*13*

a. To countries eligible for ODA.

ODA net disbursements
At constant 2013 prices and exchange rates and as a share of GNI

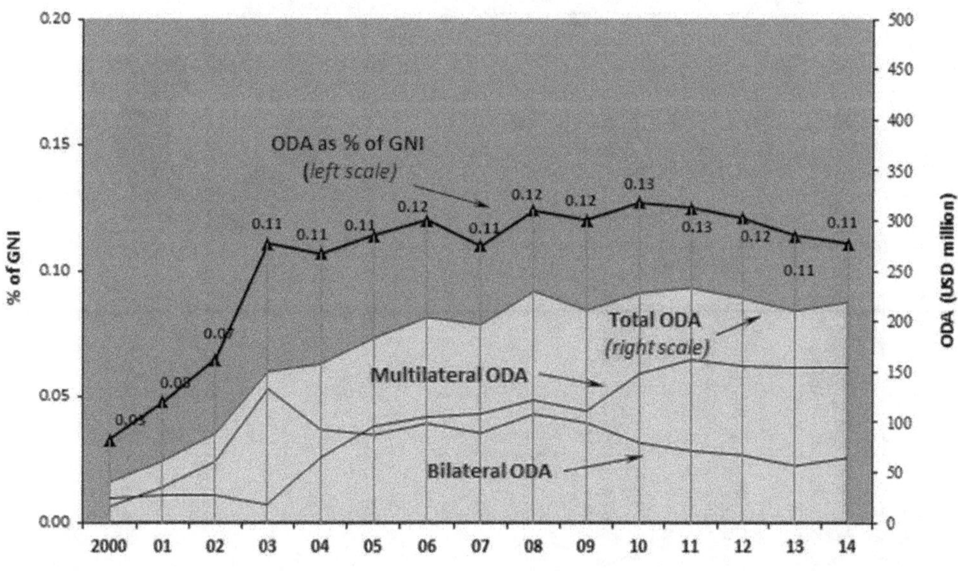

Table A.2 ODA by main categories

Disbursements

Czech Republic	Constant 2013 USD million					Per cent share of gross disbursements					Total DAC
	2010	2011	2012	2013	2014	2010	2011	2012	2013	2014	2014%
Gross Bilateral ODA	80	72	67	57	65	35	31	30	27	29	72
Budget support	1	-	-	0	1	0	-	-	0	0	2
of which: General budget support	0	-	-	-	-	0	-	-	-	-	1
Core contributions & pooled prog.& funds	1	2	3	4	3	0	1	1	2	1	14
of which: Core support to national NGOs	1	-	0	-	0	0	-	0	-	0	1
Core support to international NGOs	-	1	1	1	1	-	0	0	0	0	1
Core support to PPPs	-	0	-	0	0	-	0	-	0	0	0
Project-type interventions	30	32	32	26	31	13	14	15	12	14	40
of which: Investment projects	19	-	10	4	1	8	-	4	2	1	14
Experts and other technical assistance	23	14	12	6	6	10	6	5	3	3	4
Scholarships and student costs in donor countrie	6	5	5	5	5	3	2	2	3	2	2
of which: Imputed student costs	0	-	-	0	0	0	-	-	0	0	1
Debt relief grants	-	-	-	-	-	-	-	-	-	-	1
Administrative costs	5	6	5	5	5	2	3	2	2	2	4
Other in-donor expenditures	14	13	11	11	13	6	5	5	5	6	5
of which: refugees in donor countries	14	11	10	9	12						
Gross Multilateral ODA	149	162	156	154	155	65	69	70	73	71	28
UN agencies	6	8	8	10	10	3	3	4	5	5	5
EU institutions	111	133	120	118	132	48	57	54	56	60	9
World Bank group	11	15	17	8	8	5	6	8	4	4	6
Regional development banks	13	5	5	4	-	6	2	2	2	-	3
Other multilateral	7	1	6	14	5	3	0	3	7	2	6
Total gross ODA	228	233	223	211	219	100	100	100	100	100	100
of which: Gross ODA loans	-	-	-	-	-	-	-	-	-	-	12
Bilateral	-	-	-	-	-	-	-	-	-	-	12
Multilateral	-	-	-	-	-	-	-	-	-	-	0
Repayments and debt cancellation	-	-	-	-	-						
Total net ODA	228	233	223	211	219						
For reference:											
Free standing technical co-operation	-	0	16	12	14						
Net debt relief	-	-	-	-	-						

ODA flows to multilateral agencies, 2014

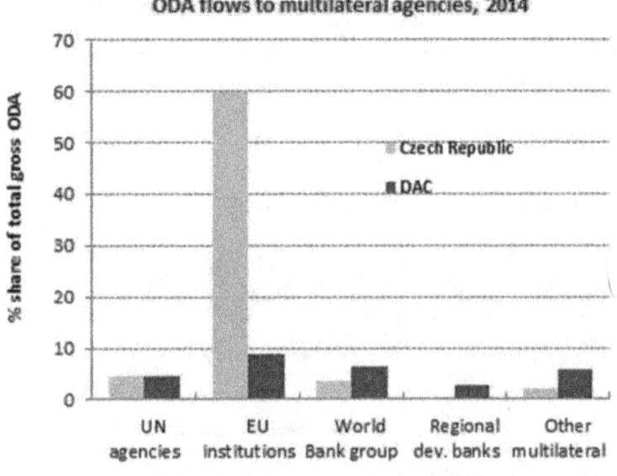

Composition of bilateral ODA, 2014, gross bilateral disbursements

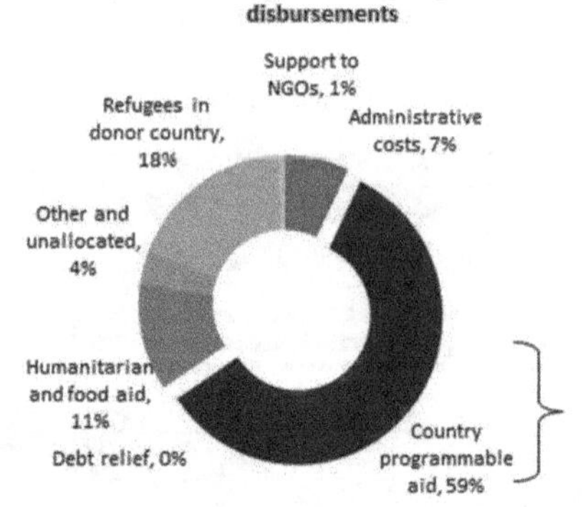

Share of ODA channelled to and through the multilateral system, two year average

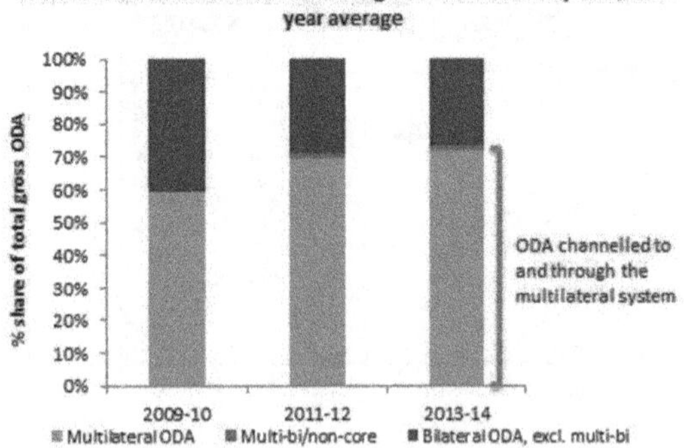

Table A.3 Bilateral ODA allocable by region and income group

Gross disbursements

Czech Republic	Constant 2013 USD million					% share					Total DAC
	2010	2011	2012	2013	2014	2010	2011	2012	2013	2014	2014%
Africa	8	9	9	7	8	11	16	15	15	14	41
Sub-Saharan Africa	8	8	7	7	7	11	13	12	13	13	35
North Africa	1	1	2	1	1	1	2	3	1	1	4
Asia	34	24	26	17	17	48	42	44	35	30	33
South and Central Asia	24	16	19	10	11	33	29	32	20	20	19
Far East	10	7	7	7	6	14	13	12	14	10	12
America	6	2	1	1	1	8	3	2	3	2	10
North and Central America	4	1	1	1	1	6	2	1	2	1	4
South America	2	1	0	1	0	2	1	1	1	1	5
Middle East	3	3	5	5	5	4	5	8	11	8	10
Oceania	0	-	-	0	-	0	-	-	0	-	2
Europe	21	19	19	18	26	29	33	32	37	46	5
Total bilateral allocable by region	72	56	60	49	57	100	100	100	100	100	100
Least developed	25	20	22	12	15	34	36	37	26	27	40
Other low-income	1	0	1	0	0	1	1	1	1	0	4
Lower middle-income	31	21	24	22	28	43	39	42	48	52	35
Upper middle-income	15	13	12	11	11	21	24	20	25	20	21
More advanced developing countries	0	-	-	-	-	1	-	-	-	-	-
Total bilateral allocable by income	72	55	58	46	54	100	100	100	100	100	100
For reference:											
Total bilateral	80	72	67	57	65	*100*	*100*	*100*	*100*	*100*	*100*
of which: Unallocated by region	*7*	*15*	*7*	*8*	*7*	*9*	*21*	*11*	*13*	*11*	*27*
of which: Unallocated by income	*8*	*17*	*9*	*11*	*10*	*10*	*24*	*14*	*19*	*16*	*36*

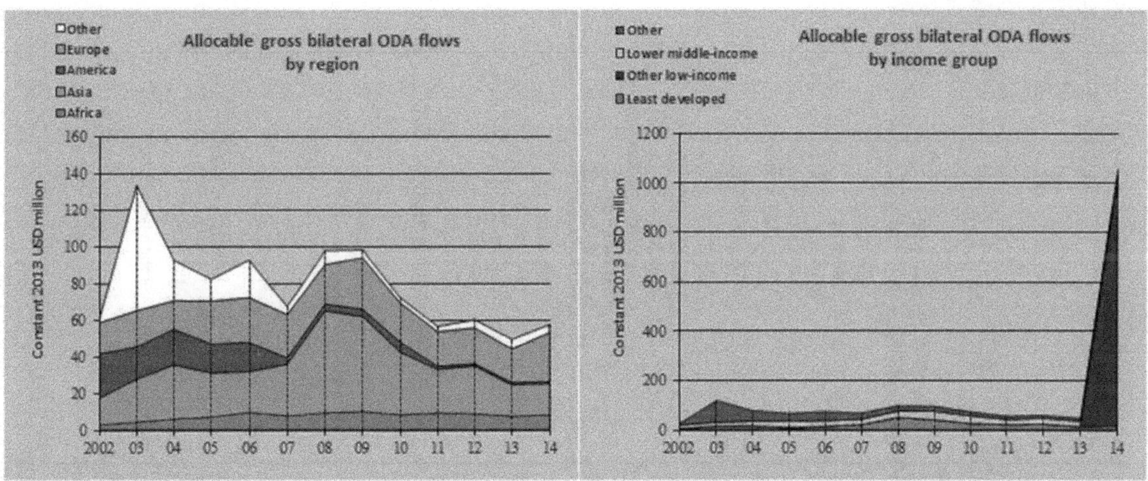

1. Each region includes regional amounts which cannot be allocated by sub-region. The sum of the sub-regional amounts may therefore fall short of the regional total.

Table A.4 Main recipients of bilateral ODA

Gross disbursements

Czech Republic	2003-07 average			Memo: DAC countries' average %		2008-12 average			Memo: DAC countries' average %		2013-14 average			Memo: DAC countries average %
	Current USD million	Constant 2013 USD mln	% share			Current USD million	Constant 2013 USD mln	% share			Current USD million	Constant 2013 USD mln	% share	
Iraq	15	23	20		Afghanistan	21	20	24		Ukraine	6	6	9	
Serbia	7	9	9		Mongolia	6	6	6		Afghanistan	5	5	8	
Afghanistan	6	8	8		Serbia	4	4	5		Moldova	5	5	8	
Mongolia	3	4	4		Moldova	4	4	4		Ethiopia	4	4	6	
Viet Nam	2	3	3		Bosnia and Herzegovina	4	4	4		Bosnia and Herzegovina	4	4	6	
Top 5 recipients	**33**	**46**	**44**	**31**	**Top 5 recipients**	**39**	**37**	**44**	**31**	**Top 5 recipients**	**22**	**23**	**37**	**23**
Bosnia and Herzegovina	2	3	3		Ukraine	3	3	4		Mongolia	3	3	5	
Ukraine	2	2	3		Georgia	3	3	4		Georgia	3	3	5	
Moldova	1	2	2		Viet Nam	3	3	3		Kosovo	2	2	3	
China (People's Republic of)	1	2	2		West Bank and Gaza Strip	2	2	2		Syrian Arab Republic	2	2	3	
Indonesia	1	1	2		Kosovo	2	2	2		Serbia	2	2	3	
Top 10 recipients	**41**	**57**	**55**	**41**	**Top 10 recipients**	**52**	**50**	**59**	**45**	**Top 10 recipients**	**34**	**34**	**56**	**36**
Pakistan	1	1	1		Ethiopia	2	2	2		Viet Nam	1	1	2	
Belarus	1	1	1		Angola	2	2	2		Belarus	1	1	2	
Georgia	1	1	1		Belarus	2	2	2		Cambodia	1	1	2	
Yemen	1	1	1		Myanmar	1	1	1		Armenia	1	1	2	
Angola	1	1	1		Cambodia	1	1	1		Myanmar	1	1	1	
Top 15 recipients	**44**	**62**	**60**	**46**	**Top 15 recipients**	**59**	**57**	**67**	**51**	**Top 15 recipients**	**39**	**40**	**65**	**42**
Namibia	1	1	1		Zambia	1	1	1		West Bank and Gaza Strip	1	1	1	
Ethiopia	1	1	1		Kazakhstan	1	1	1		Zambia	1	1	1	
Albania	1	1	1		Yemen	1	1	1		Cuba	1	1	1	
Kyrgyzstan	1	1	1		Turkey	1	1	1		Turkey	0	0	1	
Sri Lanka	0	1	1		Pakistan	1	1	1		Iraq	0	0	1	
Top 20 recipients	**47**	**66**	**64**	**51**	**Top 20 recipients**	**64**	**61**	**72**	**56**	**Top 20 recipients**	**42**	**43**	**70**	**46**
Total (116 recipients)	**58**	**80**	**79**		**Total (115 recipients)**	**78**	**75**	**88**		**Total (106 recipients)**	**50**	**51**	**83**	
Unallocated	15	20	21	33	Unallocated	10	10	12	31	Unallocated	10	10	17	38
Total bilateral gross	**73**	**100**	**100**	**100**	**Total bilateral gross**	**88**	**85**	**100**	**100**	**Total bilateral gross**	**60**	**61**	**100**	**100**

Table A.5 Bilateral ODA by major purposes

at constant 2011 prices and exchange rates

Gross disbursements - Two-year average

Czech Republic	2003-07 average		2008-12 average		2013-14 average		2013-14
	2013 USD million	%	2013 USD million	%	2013 USD million	%	%
Social infrastructure & services	39	39	45	55	27	47	38
Education	8	8	9	11	10	17	8
of which: basic education	0	0	1	1	1	1	2
Health	11	11	3	4	3	5	5
of which: basic health	9	9	0	1	1	2	3
Population & reproductive health	0	0	0	0	0	0	7
Water supply & sanitation	4	4	7	8	5	8	4
Government & civil society	14	14	23	28	8	13	11
of which: Conflict, peace & security	8	8	18	22	3	4	2
Other social infrastructure & services	2	2	3	4	2	3	2
Economic infrastructure & services	4	4	5	6	3	5	19
Transport & storage	2	2	1	1	-	-	8
Communications	0	0	0	0	-	-	0
Energy	3	3	3	4	2	4	7
Banking & financial services	0	0	0	0	-	-	2
Business & other services	0	0	0	0	0	1	2
Production sectors	6	6	7	9	6	9	7
Agriculture, forestry & fishing	3	3	5	6	4	8	5
Industry, mining & construction	3	3	2	3	1	2	1
Trade & tourism	0	0	0	0	0	0	1
Multisector	13	13	2	3	2	3	9
Commodity and programme aid	0	0	0	0	-	-	3
Action relating to debt	15	15	1	1	-	-	2
Humanitarian aid	7	7	5	6	6	10	11
Administrative costs of donors	5	5	5	6	5	8	6
Refugees in donor countries	10	10	12	14	10	18	5
Total bilateral allocable	99	100	82	100	59	100	100
For reference:							
Total bilateral	*100*	*56*	*85*	*38*	*61*	*28*	*73*
of which: Unallocated	*1*	*1*	*3*	*1*	*3*	*1*	*1*
Total multilateral	*78*	*44*	*140*	*62*	*154*	*72*	*27*
Total ODA	***178***	***100***	***225***	***100***	***216***	***100***	***100***

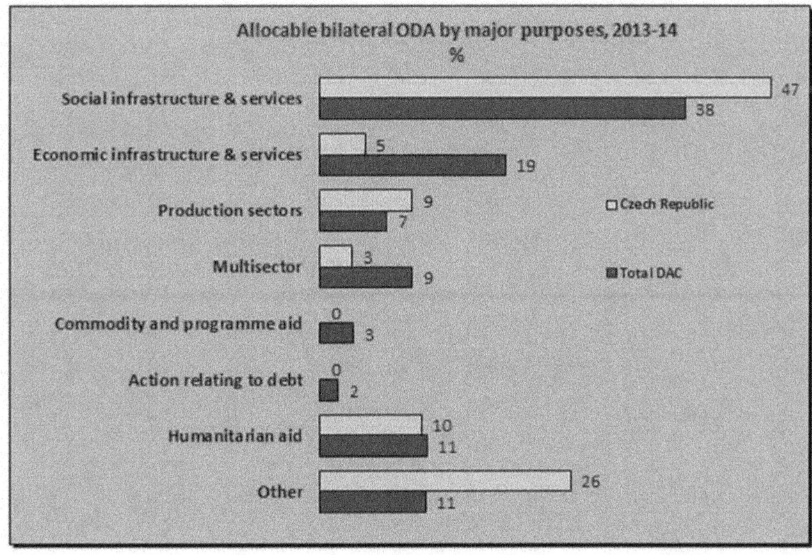

Table A.6 Comparative aid performance

	Official development assistance			Net disbursements: Share of multilateral aid				Grant element of ODA commitments	*Commitments*: Untied aid % of bilateral commitments
	2014		2008-09 to 2013-14 Average annual % change in real terms	2014				2014	Year
				% of ODA		% of GNI			
	USD million	% of GNI		(b)	(c)	(b)	(c)	% (a)	(d)
Australia	4 382	0.31	4.5	20.2		0.06		99.9	89.1
Austria	1 235	0.28	-3.5	48.4	23.1	0.14	0.07	100.0	48.2
Belgium	2 448	0.46	-1.4	46.0	25.2	0.21	0.12	99.9	96.7
Canada	4 240	0.24	-1.6	22.7		0.05		97.2	93.0
Czech Republic	212	0.11	-0.5	70.5	10.6	0.08	0.01	100.0	32.4
Denmark	3 003	0.86	0.7	29.0	19.9	0.25	0.17	100.0	95.1
Finland	1 635	0.60	4.0	42.6	30.6	0.26	0.18	100.0	90.4
France	10 620	0.37	-1.0	38.7	16.5	0.14	0.06	85.6	92.3
Germany	16 566	0.42	3.2	30.0	12.7	0.13	0.05	83.6	83.6
Greece	247	0.11	-16.8	81.4	8.1	0.09	0.01	100.0	22.0
Iceland	37	0.22	-3.5	17.1		0.04		100.0	100.0
Ireland	816	0.38	-5.2	36.4	18.8	0.14	0.07	100.0	98.0
Italy	4 009	0.19	-1.7	65.8	24.3	0.12	0.05	99.9	93.7
Japan	9 266	0.19	3.4	35.1		0.07		87.0	78.1
Korea	1 857	0.13	13.1	24.8		0.03		95.1	53.2
Luxembourg	423	1.06	-1.0	29.0	20.9	0.31	0.22	100.0	97.5
Netherlands	5 573	0.64	-3.4	27.7	16.1	0.18	0.10	100.0	98.4
New Zealand	506	0.27	1.4	19.2		0.05		100.0	81.8
Norway	5 086	1.00	2.7	23.5		0.24		100.0	100.0
Poland	452	0.09	5.2	81.8	6.7	0.07	0.01	90.0	10.6
Portugal	430	0.19	-3.4	42.7	4.0	0.08	0.01	89.7	34.5
Slovak Republic	83	0.09	0.6	80.3	6.9	0.07	0.01	100.0	0.0
Slovenia	62	0.12	-1.8	67.1	11.5	0.08	0.01	100.0	
Spain	1 877	0.13	-19.8	75.3	20.7	0.10	0.03	100.0	83.6
Sweden	6 233	1.09	2.8	30.3	23.8	0.33	0.26	100.0	85.8
Switzerland	3 522	0.50	5.4	21.1		0.11		100.0	93.9
United Kingdom	19 306	0.70	9.0	41.8	31.9	0.29	0.22	98.9	99.9
United States	33 096	0.19	1.5	16.9		0.03		100.0	62.5
Total DAC	**137 222**	**0.30**	**1.4**	**31.0**		**0.09**		**94.2**	**80.6**
Memo: **Average country effort**		**0.39**							

Notes:

a. **Excluding debt reorganisation.**

b. **Including EU institutions.**

c. **Excluding EU institutions.**

d. **Excluding administrative costs and in-donor refugee costs.**

.. **Data not available.**

Figure A.1 Net ODA from DAC countries in 2015 (preliminary figures)

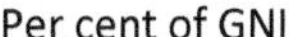

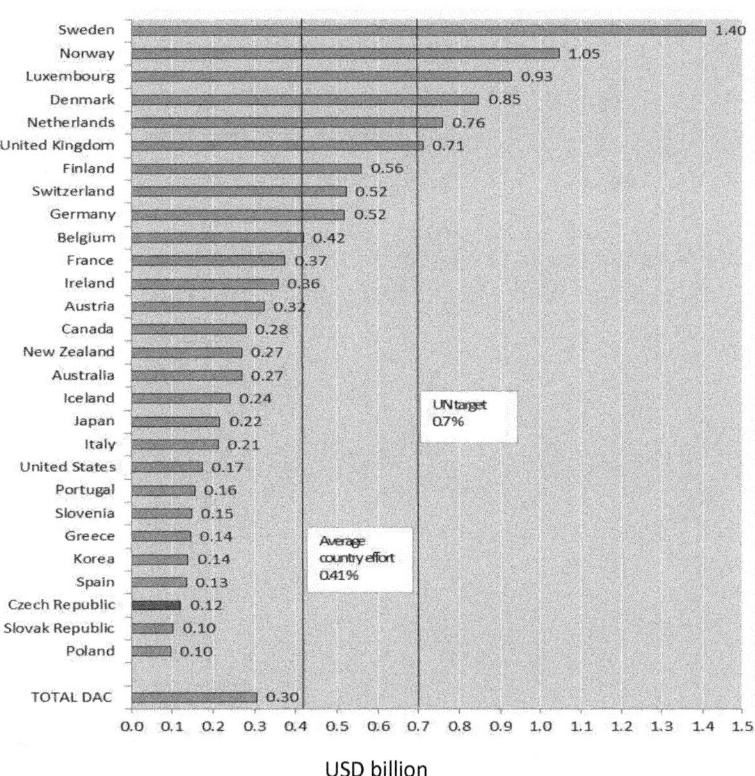

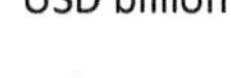

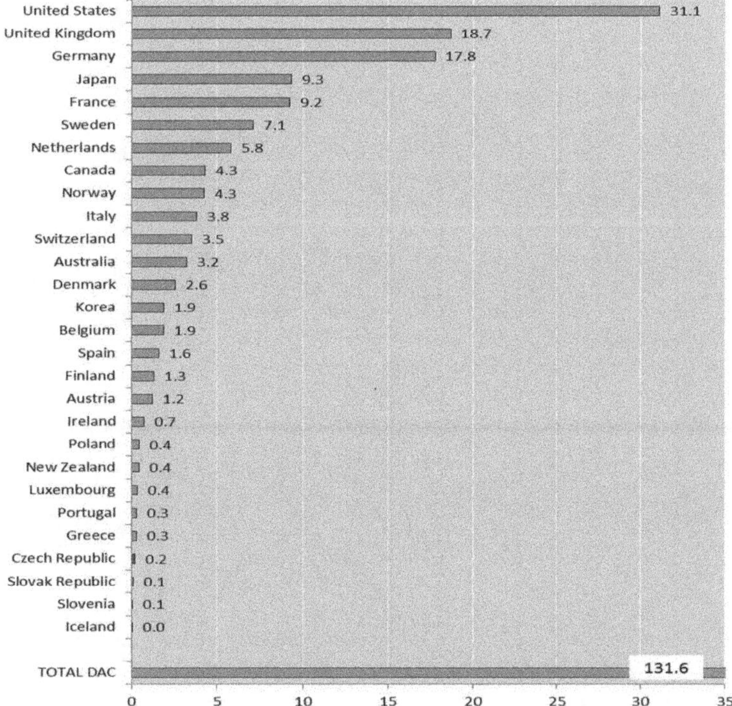

Annex B: Organisational structure

Figure B.1 The Czech Republic aid system

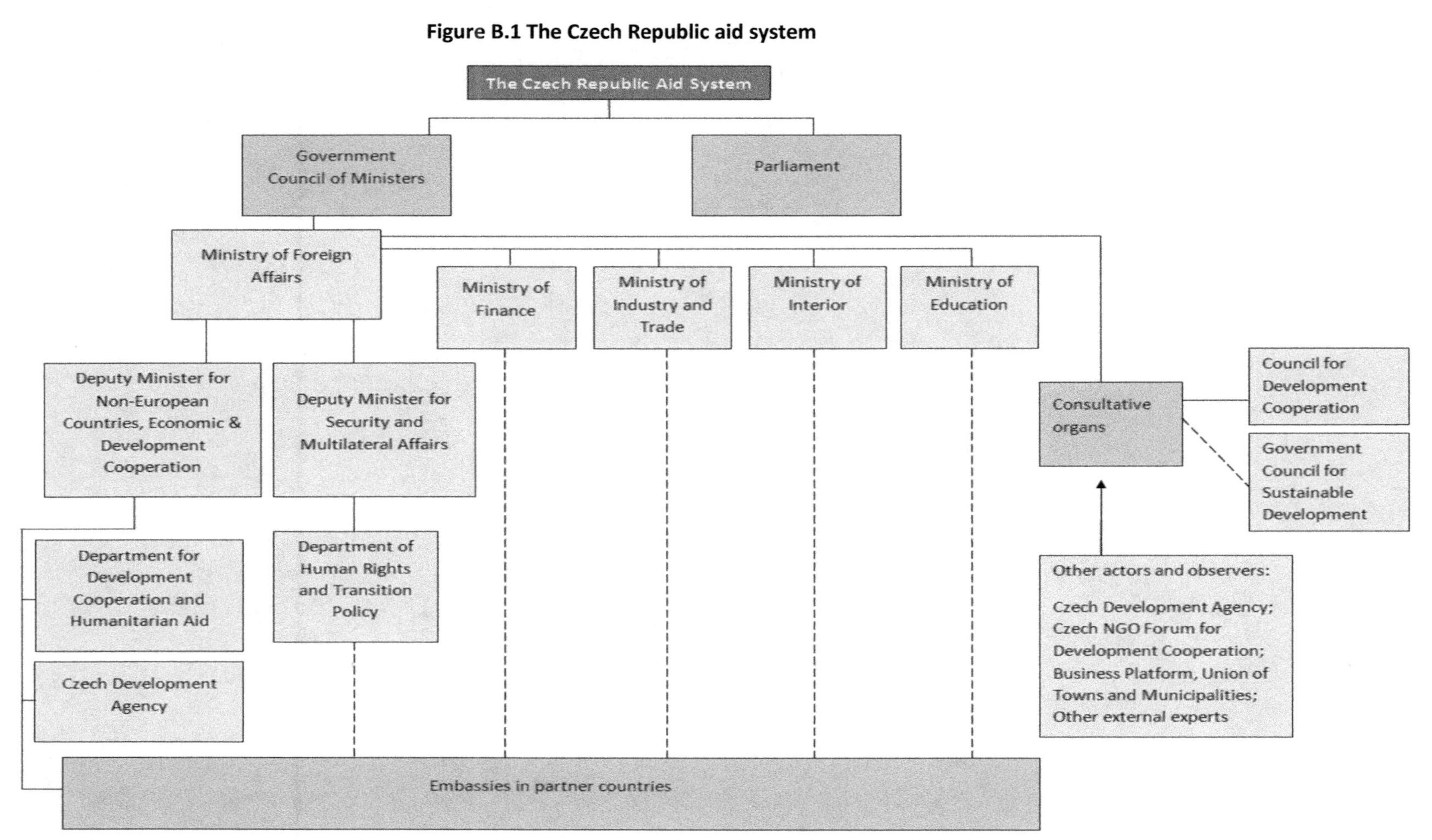

Annex C: Perspectives from Ethiopia and Moldova on Czech development co-operation

The Czech Republic's development co-operation is centrally managed and has, to date, a limited physical presence in partner countries or territories. To get a perspective on how the Czech Republic delivers its development co-operation in its programme countries, the peer review team held meetings in Prague with the Czech ambassadors and development diplomats based in Ethiopia and Moldova as well as the relevant managers in the Czech Development Agency and the Ministry of Foreign Affairs. The team organised follow-up phone interviews with eight partners – partner government and non-governmental organisations – to deepen the field perspective.

The Czech Republic's policies, strategies and aid allocations to Ethiopia and Moldova

Support to Ethiopia builds on a history of co-operation and has a regional focus

The Czech Republic has been providing ODA to Ethiopia since 2001. Historically, Ethiopia was a significant trade partner with the former Czechoslovakia. Since 2001, the Czech Republic has been scaling up its support and making it more strategic. Ethiopia became a "programme country" for Czech Development Cooperation in 2012. In its 2012-2017 Development Cooperation Programme for Ethiopia, the Czech Republic prioritises five sectors: education; health; water supply and sanitation; agriculture; and forestry and fishing – as well as disaster prevention and preparedness (MFA, 2012). It also provides scholarships to Ethiopian students – typically on subjects related to its focus areas. This programme is an integral part of the memorandum of understanding between the Czech Ministry of Foreign Affairs and the Ministry of Finance and Economic Development of the Federal Democratic Republic of Ethiopia.

According to the most recent Development Assistance Committee (DAC) data, the Czech Republic disbursed on average USD 3.4 million annually to Ethiopia between 2012 and 2014 (Figure C.1). This is the equivalent to about 0.18% of total net ODA to Ethiopia over the period. The Czech Republic focuses on the Southern Nations, Nationalities and Peoples' Region (SNNPR) in Ethiopia. Given the relatively small size of its aid budget, it has prioritised a few *woreda* (districts) in SNNPR in close co-operation with local authorities. It chose this region also in order to capitalise on the local knowledge and experience of the Czech non-governmental organisation (NGO) People in Need, which was implementing its own projects in the region prior to the arrival of Czech ODA. People in Need also implements projects financed with Czech ODA.

The Czech Republic's humanitarian assistance to Ethiopia has focused mainly on the Somali National Regional State but also on SNNPR, Oromia and Gambella (support to South-Sudanese refugees and local hosting communities).

Figure C.1 Czech ODA disbursements to Ethiopia and Moldova and total bilateral ODA, 2004-2014

Gross disbursements, million USD

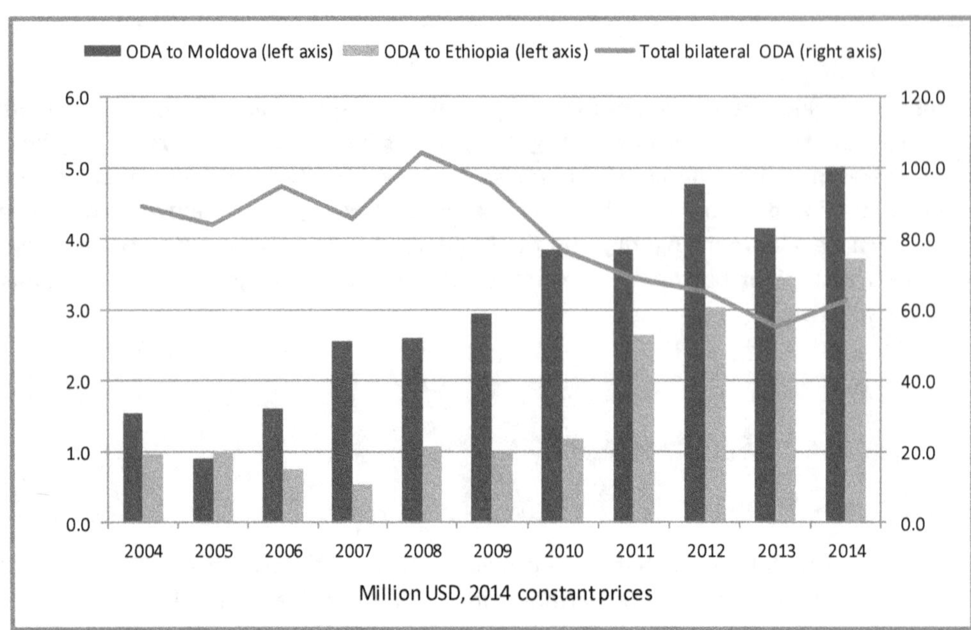

Source: OECD (2016), "Geographical distribution of financial flows: Flows to developing countries", OECD International Development Statistics (database), DOI: http://dx.doi.org/10.1787/data-00566-en (Accessed on 05 July 2016)

Czech support in Moldova focuses on vulnerability and sharing transition experiences

Moldova has been a key partner for Czech development co-operation since 2008. As an Eastern Partnership Country transitioning to a market economy, Moldova can benefit from the Czech Republic's own transition experience and reform expertise. The Czech Republic is one of the largest bilateral providers in Moldova. It has four priority sectors: social infrastructure and services, water supply and sanitation, agriculture and environmental protection as well as support of the state and civil society (MFA, 2011). Moldova already benefited from Czech experience with economic transition and implementation of EU *acquis communautaire* through a technical assistance project focused on legislation and administration of public finances (MFA, 2011). In the agriculture sector, the Czech Republic is helping Moldova to establish a vineyard register in line with EU standards. The Czech Republic co-operates actively with international organisations based in Moldova and bilateral providers such as Austria, Germany, Slovakia, Switzerland and the United States of America.

According to the most recent DAC data, the Czech Republic disbursed on average USD 5 million annually to Moldova between 2012 and 2014 (Figure C.1). This is the equivalent of about 0.58% of total net ODA to Moldova over the period. The Czech Republic has good relations with the partner government and with the local authorities. It has a deep understanding of the government system and can play a role at the institutional level by supporting reforms. In addition, it has a long-term perspective in certain sectors (e.g. in supporting social care and home assistance) and specific expertise (e.g. in wine registration) that is valued by Moldova. The Czech Development Agency, Czech line ministries and the embassy all implement activities in Moldova. The Agency mainly implements bilateral projects through Czech partners and their local implementing partners and provides expertise in project and programme monitoring. The embassy has taken steps to reduce the administrative costs of managing small grants by increasing their minimum size.

A learning-by-doing approach feeds into planning and project cycle management

The Czech Republic has improved its project planning thanks, in part, to the project-cycle management methodology which was developed in 2011. In addition, it has introduced more rigour and evidence into project-cycle management. Mid-term reviews of the country programmes and solid evaluations of Czech projects provide useful information about strengths and weaknesses. There is also an appetite to learn from practice and to use this knowledge to improve quality.

Programming at country level is still work in progress: there is scope to improve the Czech Republic's already good knowledge of the context and needs in partner countries or territories and of the priorities and activities of other providers. This would allow the Czech Republic to increase synergies and co-ordination in a given sector, to find its niche and ensure added value in programme-based approaches and joint projects with other providers. The Czech Republic could, for example, pilot innovative approaches in key sectors before scaling up. By increasing its capacity in partner countries or territories, as planned, it can take programming and project-cycle management to a new level. This is in line with the Czech strategic priority to focus on fewer activities for greater impact.

The Czech Republic needs to focus on fewer priorities and bigger projects

According to the DAC Creditor Reporting System, in 2014 the Czech Republic reported 37 bilateral activities in Ethiopia. The majority (21) were project-type interventions managed by CzDA and implemented by Czech NGOs, universities and private companies, a few technical assistance activities, small grants managed by the embassy and scholarships. The largest annual disbursement was about USD 430 000 (basic health infrastructure), five projects disbursed about USD 250 000, and the average disbursement was USD 100 000.

In Moldova, the Czech Republic reported 46 activities in 2014: mostly project-type interventions managed by the Agency, some by the Ministry of Foreign Affairs and technical assistance implemented by the Ministry of Finance. The largest disbursement was USD 780 000 and four activities disbursed USD 450 000, but the majority of them were under USD 100 000. The average disbursement was, as for Ethiopia, USD 100 000.

Ethiopia's Ministry of Finance and Economic Development (MoFED) has, for example, highlighted the need for greater focus and bigger projects to achieve better impact in its feedback to the embassy. In response, the CzDA has set a minimum project level of USD 500 000. The Government of Ethiopia suggested that the Czech Republic focus on two sectors in the next country strategy – agriculture and water. Ethiopia would also like the Czech Republic to engage in pooled funding and direct capacity building with local authorities. The Czech Republic is considering the options available to fulfil this demand.

Similarly to Ethiopia, the government of Moldova would value bigger projects and programmes to move beyond individual sites to achieve regional coverage. While the country strategy offers the potential for good guidance, the sectoral focus is too broad. The Czech Republic could reduce the number of sectors and increase the size of its projects.

Capping the number of small grants can increase efficiency

Small grants are a useful tool for embassies to raise the Czech Republic's profile. These grants are more flexible than other instruments because they can be transferred directly to local partners. However, given the small size of the budget for these grants, their scope for development impact is low. At the same time, there is a risk that development diplomats spend a disproportionate amount of time in identifying, setting up and administering these grants. In 2015, the guidelines for project identification, reporting and financial control were reviewed and updated. To increase efficiency, the embassy in Moldova decided to cap the number of grants to three per year, with a minimum amount of about CZK 500 000 per grant (about EUR 18 000).

Organisation and management

Embassies' important role is limited by capacity constraints

In both Ethiopia and Moldova the embassies play an important role, working with the government to identify country needs and priorities and discuss project ideas. Collaboration and co-ordination between the embassies and the Agency work well.

The embassies face capacity constraints, however. In Moldova, the development diplomat can only spend up to 50% of her time on development co-operation and the rest on economic diplomacy. Development time is spent engaging with the government to identify project ideas, supporting the government's submission of project proposals, coordinating with other development partners, managing the small grant scheme, approving business-to-business projects, monitoring the Agency's projects, supporting implementing partners and connecting them with government. The monitoring aspect of the job (up to 30 projects) is proving difficult to deliver in this resource constrained situation.

To ease the workload, both embassies have hired local staff to work specifically on development issues: one full-time staff member in Ethiopia and one full-time and one part-time in Moldova. The work of local staff is very valuable since they bring institutional knowledge, they can relate easily with local partners and in some instances have experience in project management. While language does not seem to be a working constraint because local staff may draft monitoring reports in Czech or English, local co-ordinators and development diplomats would gain from having access to training on specific aspects of development co-operation.

Deploying CzDA staff to Ethiopia and Moldova will reinforce capacity to deliver the programme

Deploying Czech Development Agency staff in the field would ease capacity and skill constraints and speed up project approval, annual contracts and disbursements. With adequate delegated authority, the Agency could bring value through its technical expertise in programming, implementation and monitoring. This would free up capacity in the embassy, allowing it to deepen policy dialogue with the government and partners through its better understanding of the local context. At the same time, decentralising authority over operations to the field level is expensive. Levels of decentralisation should be proportional to the size of the programme.

Partnerships, results and accountability

The Czech Republic participates in EU joint programming, and plays a leadership role when capacity permits

The Czech Republic emphasises the importance of partnering with national and local government and responding to local needs. Given the relatively small size of its project and rules that generally require Czech "entities"' to implement projects (Chapter 5), it focuses on local-level projects where it can make a difference and which give it some visibility. While it does not work through government systems in Ethiopia, it collaborates closely with government authorities in the SNNPR region and co-operates with the Ministry of Finance and Economic Development.

The Czech Embassy in Ethiopia participates, when relevant, in donor co-ordination meetings in Addis Ababa – especially EU meetings – but it does not participate in joint projects. In the SNNPR region where it implements its projects, it is harder to co-ordinate with other donors since the embassy is not physically present in the region and it is difficult to get information from regional government on what other providers are doing.

In Moldova, the embassy is active in donor co-ordination meetings and participates in EU joint programming. In particular, it contributes to joint analysis carried out by sectoral working groups in the sectors that are relevant for its projects. Thanks to its expertise and close co-operation with the Moldovan government, the Czech Republic leads the working group in charge of social development, including social policy and health.

Pilots for planning and monitoring programme results are underway

From 2017, the CzDA aims to introduce results-based management into all new programmes with partner countries or territories rather than just in individual projects. To prepare for this transition, in 2015 the CzDA developed two pilot sector programmes – water and sanitation in Moldova and agriculture in Ethiopia – which include measurable indicators. For example, the overall aim of the pilot programme for the agricultural sector in Ethiopia is to "improve the management of natural resources and support sustainable livelihoods of small farmers in SNNPR". It includes an overall measurable indicator (verifiable using statistics from local agricultural offices).

Local implementing partners could receive better feedback

Implementing organisations provide semi-annual monitoring reports to the CzDA – the Agency releases new tranches of financing based on these. The Agency recognises that reporting templates could be more straightforward and results-oriented. The reports should be shared more systematically with partners. This is not the case at present, although informal feedback meetings are usually organised at the end of CzDA monitoring visits.

Bibliography

Government sources

MFA (2012), *Development Cooperation Programme, Ethiopia, 2012-2017*, Ministry of Foreign Affairs, Prague, www.mzv.cz/file/940755/TISK_Program_Etiopie__anglictina_.pdf.

MFA (2011), *Development Cooperation Programme, Moldova, 2011-2017*, Ministry of Foreign Affairs, Prague www.mzv.cz/file/962031/Development_coop_programme_MD_2011_2017.pdf.

ORGANISATION FOR ECONOMIC CO-OPERATION AND DEVELOPMENT

The OECD is a unique forum where governments work together to address the economic, social and environmental challenges of globalisation. The OECD is also at the forefront of efforts to understand and to help governments respond to new developments and concerns, such as corporate governance, the information economy and the challenges of an ageing population. The Organisation provides a setting where governments can compare policy experiences, seek answers to common problems, identify good practice and work to co-ordinate domestic and international policies.

The OECD member countries are: Australia, Austria, Belgium, Canada, Chile, the Czech Republic, Denmark, Estonia, Finland, France, Germany, Greece, Hungary, Iceland, Ireland, Israel, Italy, Japan, Korea, Latvia, Luxembourg, Mexico, the Netherlands, New Zealand, Norway, Poland, Portugal, the Slovak Republic, Slovenia, Spain, Sweden, Switzerland, Turkey, the United Kingdom and the United States. The European Union takes part in the work of the OECD.

OECD Publishing disseminates widely the results of the Organisation's statistics gathering and research on economic, social and environmental issues, as well as the conventions, guidelines and standards agreed by its members.

DEVELOPMENT ASSISTANCE COMMITTEE

To achieve its aims, the OECD has set up a number of specialised committees. One of these is the Development Assistance Committee (DAC), whose mandate is to promote development co-operation and other policies so as to contribute to sustainable development - including pro-poor economic growth, poverty reduction and the improvement of living standards in developing countries - and to a future in which no country will depend on aid. To this end, the DAC has grouped the world's main donors, defining and monitoring global standards in key areas of development.

The members of the DAC are Australia, Austria, Belgium, Canada, the Czech Republic, Denmark, the European Union, Finland, France, Germany, Greece, Iceland, Ireland, Italy, Japan, Korea, Luxembourg, the Netherlands, New Zealand, Norway, Poland, Portugal, the Slovak Republic, Slovenia, Spain, Sweden, Switzerland, the United Kingdom and the United States.

The DAC issues guidelines and reference documents in the DAC Guidelines and Reference Series to inform and assist members in the conduct of their development co-operation programmes.

OECD PUBLISHING, 2, rue André-Pascal, 75775 PARIS CEDEX 16
(43 2016 061 P) ISBN 978-92-64-26492-2 – 2016

www.ingramcontent.com/pod-product-compliance
Lightning Source LLC
LaVergne TN
LVHW081417110826
845149LV00010B/1776

* 9 7 8 9 2 6 4 2 6 4 9 2 2 *